THE
DIAMOND
REVOLUTION

Also by Neil J. Sullivan

The Dodgers Move West
The Minors

THE DIAMOND REVOLUTION

THE PROSPECTS FOR BASEBALL AFTER THE COLLAPSE OF ITS RULING CLASS

Neil J. Sullivan

ST. MARTIN'S PRESS
NEW YORK

Design by Erich Hobbing

Library of Congress Cataloging-in-Publication Data

Sullivan, Neil J., 1948–
    The diamond revolution: the prospects for baseball after the collapse of its ruling
class / Neil J. Sullivan.
      p. cm
    ISBN 0-312-07723-8
    1. Baseball—United States—History.   2. Baseball—Social aspects—
United States. I. Title.
GV863.A1S893 1992   92-3629
796.357′0973—dc20   CIP

First Edition: July 1992

10 9 8 7 6 5 4 3 2 1

To John and Gertrude Sullivan

Contents

Preface

For many baseball fans, a tiresome procession of economic, legal, and social battles has disrupted their love for the game. Modern baseball features addictions, lawsuits, and labor strife as much as home runs and no-hitters. In the past, it seemed that players performed for the joy of competition, owners stayed in the background, and fans did not need advanced degrees to read the sports pages.

The good old days, of course, were not nearly so simple as we would like to believe, and a quick review of some familiar subjects makes the point:

• *Racism*—The arrival of Jackie Robinson in Brooklyn in 1947 triggered a vicious and ugly reaction. Black cats and watermelons were familiar props in opposing dugouts, while the front offices were more discreet but often just as racist. Clubs like the Yankees and the Red Sox dragged their feet on integration throughout most of the 1950s, passing up players like Willie Mays and Henry Aaron.

• *Labor Strife*—After World War II, Stan Musial was one of the players who, lured by the bounty of the Pasquel brothers, considered bolting for Mexico. The Mexican option was the first chance at a free market for players since the Federal League operated during World War I, but the major league owners cracked the whip and held their star players in the bonds of the reserve clause.

• *Litigation*—In the early 1950s, George Toolson of the New York Yankees rebelled at being sent to the minor leagues. He went to court to win the same right to choose his employer that any other American worker had. He lost as the Supreme Court upheld the plantation labor policies of the major league owners.

• *Congressional Hearings*—The Toolson case helped trigger congressional investigations of baseball's antitrust status. These proved to be little more than an exercise in theatrics for the politicians, but some interesting questions were raised before they were ducked.

• *Gambling*—A headline story when Pete Rose was in short pants. Leo Durocher had not bet on baseball, but he kept company with some Damon Runyon characters who offended the sensibilities of some of baseball's rulers. In a period of feudal justice, Durocher was suspended for the 1947 season.

• *Franchise Moves*—The Athletics, the Braves, and the Browns fled for their commercial lives in the early 1950s when Philadelphia, Boston, and St. Louis seemed to support only one team. A few years later, the Dodgers and the Giants left for California, leaving a bitterness that still lingers in the hearts of many New Yorkers.

• *Expansion*—Frustrated with the complacency of the American and National leagues, Branch Rickey formed the Continental League in 1960 to bring major league baseball to cities like Atlanta, Buffalo, Denver, and Toronto. The teams existed only on paper and in the dreams of civic boosters, but the threat triggered the major league expansion of the 1960s and 1970s.

This sample of controversies suggests that baseball has always had its business issues that have distracted from the charm of the game. The difference today is that the owners and the players have become equal, if uneasy, partners. Problems that used to be squelched on the owners' whim are now bargained or litigated in quarrelsome, public, and lengthy debates that test the patience of fans to their limits.

Today, when we most enjoy the sport of baseball, we seem to be set up for a bracing intrusion from the business of baseball. The 1991 World Series provides one example. On the Tuesday after the Series ended, the front page of the *New York Times* sports section included a column by Ira Berkow that celebrated the Series as perhaps "the best sustained sporting event anyone has ever seen."[1] Berkow put the games between the Twins and the Braves into a baseball pantheon by drawing comparisons with the World Series of 1905, 1924, 1960, 1972, and 1975. He mentioned the heroics of Christy Mathewson, Walter Johnson, and Bill Mazeroski—fairly accessible references to a baseball fan. Without becoming maudlin, Berkow placed the 1991 World Series in its proper emotional setting in the game's history.

Three columns to the right on the same page, Murray Chass's story led, "Less than 12 hours after winning the seventh game of the World Series and its Most Valuable Player Award, Jack Morris notified the Minnesota Twins yesterday that he would not exercise the option in his contract for 1992."[2] Chass explained the free agency intricacies of Morris's contract in an article that also discussed other established stars who might be playing for different teams in 1992.

We now seem to have less than a day to savor a thrilling World Series before we have to steel ourselves for the turmoil of the off-season. Berkow gives us baseball's romance—all the better for not being mawkish—then Chass throws a bucket of ice water to remind us that the business of this sport is constant, complicated, and contentious. What's a fan to do?

Our tendency may be to appreciate the game and to curse the business, but *The Diamond Revolution* proposes a different reaction. The business of baseball should not be seen as a new toxin that is poisoning our game. Baseball has always been shaped as much by officials in the front office as by players on the field—a point that the racial ban on black players illustrates so well. The business side of the sport has been undergoing radical upheavals, transformations that this book explains. Since the revolution in baseball is far from complete, battles among the contending factions will continue to erupt for many years to come. We can ignore or damn these changes, or we can try to understand them: Why have they arisen? How might they improve the game? What risks do these changes bring? Can fans influence the outcome in any way?

For the most part, this book is intended for fans who have been puzzled, intrigued, or aggravated by the business of baseball, but the work may also be helpful to the men and women who will more directly determine the future of the game. Several of the movers and shakers of baseball who were interviewed for this project cautioned that academics try to impose rational models on a baseball business that operates more by emotional internal politics. Fair enough, but there is, of course, a rejoinder. The rulers of baseball sometimes become so engaged in their encapsulated world that they make decisions that are oblivious to the interests of people they need. If fans, taxpayers, smaller communities, minor leagues, or other parties are indifferently abused, the pampered status of the major leagues may end abruptly.

To this point, our love of the game has been far stronger than our disgust for the business, but that simple, childlike love may not be permanent. When the front office strife concerned racial justice or fair working relations, those worthy issues could hold our attention. But if the contention in the future is simply over how to grasp the most money in the shortest time, fans cannot be expected to remain sympathetic.

More than most businesses, baseball's heritage is a tremendous resource that must be developed with care and judgment. The men and women who will guide baseball through the rest of its transition will need to resist the fool's gold that will be the reward for short-term expediency. If these leaders

Preface

decide that the highest immediate revenues are baseball's primary objective, then Fenway Park will be replaced by a domed stadium and baseball's playoffs will include wild-card teams—two proposals that were reported in the wake of the 1991 World Series.

If wiser heads prevail, tradition will be honored. Baseball's marketing executives will recognize that nothing they do promotes the game so effectively as parents taking their children to the ball park and telling the next generation about the great players, teams, and games of the past. *The Diamond Revolution* rests on the premise that how the past is understood will help to determine the history of baseball in the twenty-first century. To that point, the book concludes that the grab for quick money is a path to ruin for baseball, while respect for the heritage of the game is the way to even greater prosperity.

NOTES

1. *New York Times*, October 29, 1991, p. B7.
2. Ibid.

Acknowledgments

The people interviewed for this book not only provided valuable information and corrected some of my more egregious sins, but they were all generous and gracious to have taken time away from their own work to help me with mine. They are listed in the bibliography, and each of them has my sincere appreciation.

Professor Mel Dubnick has borne my fascination with baseball with all the grace one could hope from his department's chair. Other academics who have offered their encouragement include Bill Agee, Rob Baade, Fred Roberts, and Ron Yoshida. The best lessons are taught by example, and no student ever received better guidance than that provided by my mentor, Peter Woll. My understanding of business continues to grow through the help of my colleague, Dan Fenn, who sheds light on the major league owners through his knowledge of international traders and Democratic politicians.

I am most grateful to Jane Dystel, my agent, and George Witte, my editor, both of whom have been graceful in their patience and encouragement. Kathleen Ireland provided much-needed guidance through the mysteries of cable broadcasting, and Susie Freedman contributed valuable research.

Roger Hannon, Yankee fan, begins to show the strains of rooting for that franchise, adding a sense of urgency to my proposed reforms. Greg Shuker, Mets fan, has rediscovered

Acknowledgments

hope—the eternal lure of this game. Bob Fitzpatrick is a rare friend who actually admits to reading my books. Mike and Lana Sremba have extended their friendship and assistance during those research trips to California. The Reverends Dave Lockhart and Kim Jones share my fascination with baseball, but Sister Geraldine McCullagh, Mets fan, makes the key spriritual point that the game is conclusive proof that God is female.

Speaking of female deities, I remain grateful as ever to my wife, Joyce. Kate and Tim are our special blessings. Without their constant help the book would have been done months ago, and I would have missed some fascinating developments in baseball. I appreciate Barbara Trick's care of the younger Sullivans as do they. I am happy to dedicate the book to my uncle and aunt, John and Gertrude Sullivan, with much love and appreciation.

1

Remembrance
of Games Past

For those of us who have reached middle age, our appreciation for baseball is greatly affected by the unreliable glow of
our memories. Nostalgia assures us that the players of our
youth were better, the teams more exciting, and the ball
parks more enchanting. The era that so bewitches us is the
especially appealing period from 1946 to 1957. Our memories
sift those years to create a single spectacular moment:

- Ted Williams and Bob Feller lead a return from combat of
  the stars who left baseball to save America;
- Jackie Robinson breaks the color barrier;
- Joe DiMaggio reigns in New York;
- Lavagetto's clutch hit and Gionfriddo's catch in the 1947
  Series;
- Spahn and Sain and pray for rain;
- the bad call in the 1948 Series on Feller's pickoff;
- Ashburn and the Whiz Kids;
- Connie Mack departs;
- Ralph Kiner's home run titles in Forbes Field;
- Stan the Man's corkscrew stance;
- DiMaggio leaves, Mantle arrives;
- Bobby Thomson's home run;

THE DIAMOND REVOLUTION

- The Dodgers' wonderful summers and frustrating falls;
- Eddie Gaedel;
- Willie's catch on Vic Wertz;
- Leo the Lip;
- Joe Adcock's four home runs and a double;
- Trader Frank Lane;
- Herb Score;
- Campy and Yogi;
- Ernie Banks in Wrigley Field;
- Al Kaline's batting title;
- Podres's pitching, Amoros's catch, and a World Series for Brooklyn;
- Dale Long's home runs in eight consecutive games;
- Frank Robinson's rookie year;
- Casey testifying before Congress;
- Larsen's perfect game;
- Roy Sievers' home run title;
- Lew Burdette's three wins in 1957 for the Milwaukee Braves' only World Series title;
- Opening day on Monday in Cincinnati and Washington, D.C.;
- Presidents who threw out the first ball;
- and the moves of the Dodgers and the Giants, ending a golden age.

As kids we were oblivious to the business structure on which this collage of heroics rested. Challenges to the reserve clause were rare and hopeless, so they were safely ignored. Ball parks had served for decades—why would they suddenly become obsolete? The tie between a community and its team was as certain as marriage, so who would think of Brooklyn without the Dodgers? No ten-year-old today could be so innocent.

These memories leave every fan with a reason to revere the good old days, but our memories of the exciting championship battles in New York and of local heroics everywhere can dis-

2

tract us from the stagnant quality of competition in the post-war era. For a generation after World War II, a few elite teams dominated the game, largely impervious to challenges from teams that were stuck in the mire of futility, as these figures indicate:

Team Finishes, 1946–57

TEAM	FINISH BY YEARS												AVG. FIN.	PEN-NANTS
NL	46	47	48	49	50	51	52	53	54	55	56	57		
Dodgers	2	1	3	1	2	2	1	1	2	1	1	3	1.67	6
Braves	4	3	1	4	4	4	7	2	3	2	2	1	3.08	2
Cards	1	2	2	2	5	3	3	4	6	7	4	2	3.42	1
Giants	8	4	5	5	3	1	2	5	1	3	6	6	4.08	2
Phils	5	7	6	3	1	5	4	3	4	4	5	5	4.33	1
Reds	6	5	7	7	6	6	6	6	5	5	3	4	5.50	0
Cubs	3	6	8	8	7	8	5	7	7	6	8	7	6.67	0
Pirates	7	8	4	6	8	7	8	8	8	8	7	8	7.25	0
AL														
Yankees	3	1	3	1	1	1	1	1	2	1	1	1	1.42	9
Indians	6	4	1	3	4	2	2	2	1	2	2	6	2.92	2
Red Sox	1	3	2	2	3	3	6	4	4	4	4	3	3.25	1
White Sox	5	6	8	6	6	4	3	3	3	3	3	2	4.33	0
Tigers	2	2	5	4	2	5	8	6	5	5	5	4	4.42	0
Senators	4	7	7	8	5	7	5	5	6	8	7	8	6.42	0
Athletics	8	5	4	5	8	6	4	7	8	6	8	7	6.33	0
Browns/O's	7	8	6	7	7	8	7	8	7	7	6	5	6.92	0

Postwar baseball included many things for fans to appreciate, but wide-open pennant races were not among them. Not only were the titles generally confined to New York, but the truly dreadful teams could not aspire even to mediocrity. These clubs had begun to rot from the top, as their front offices lacked the imagination and determination to break out of the basement.

3

A community would not now easily accept being a locus of futility as Pittsburgh and Kansas City were in the 1950s. Fans now see franchises turned around in a year or two through the effective use of free agency. They will not sit idly through an inept decade because team officials refuse to pursue the available talent.

Not only will fans stay away from the park, but broadcast ratings can suffer, causing sponsors to give up on the franchise, dropping the team's income. Back when an entire payroll was $300,000, an owner could remain stubborn without suffering serious financial harm. But this is a different age.

The sleepy front offices of the past are largely gone. In their place are modern organizations that operate under terrific pressure to field competitive teams. Where three teams in the National League and five in the American League endured the postwar era without a pennant, in the past twelve years only the Mariners, the Rangers, and the Indians have failed to win at least division titles. The dynasties are gone, and even the doormats can dream of a quick turnaround. The figures for these past twelve years on the opposite page show this very different pattern.

Not only are the championships more evenly dispersed, but the gap between the top team and the bottom is much narrower, especially in the National League. The spread in the average finish between the Dodgers and the Braves (the best and the worst) in the NL West over the past twelve years is 1.66. In the eastern division, the Cardinals and the Cubs were an average 1.17 apart. During the postwar era, the Dodgers enjoyed a similar cushion, 1.41 places, over their next closest competitor. The span between the Dodgers and the Pirates (the best and the worst) between 1946 and 1957 was 5.58—no National League team even averages that poor a finish now.

Similar results appear in the American League if one can ignore the lamentable perennials, the Indians and the Mariners. Those have been the only two franchises that display similar patterns to the old cellar dwellers of the postwar

4

Remembrance of Games Past

Team Finishes, 1980–91

TEAM	FINISH BY YEAR												AVG.	DIV.
NL	80	81*	82	83	84	85	86	87	88	89	90	91	FIN.	TITLES
WEST														
Dodgers	2	1	2	1	4	1	5	4	1	4	2	2	2.42	4
Astros	1	2	5	3	T2	T3	1	3	5	3	4	6	3.33	2
Reds	3	3	6	6	5	2	2	2	2	5	1	5	3.50	1
Giants	5	4	3	5	6	6	3	1	4	1	3	4	3.75	2
Padres	6	6	4	4	1	T3	4	6	3	2	4	3	3.83	1
Braves	4	5	1	2	T2	5	6	5	6	6	6	1	4.08	2
EAST														
Cards	4	3	1	4	3	1	3	1	5	3	6	2	3.00	3
Mets	5	5	6	6	2	2	1	2	1	2	2	5	3.25	2
Expos	2	1	3	3	5	3	4	3	3	4	3	6	3.33	1
Phils	1	2	2	1	4	6	2	T4	6	6	4	T3	3.42	2
Pirates	3	4	4	2	6	5	6	T4	2	5	1	1	3.58	2
Cubs	6	6	5	5	1	4	5	6	4	1	4	T3	4.17	2
AL														
WEST														
Royals	1	2	2	2	1	1	T3	2	3	2	6	6	2.58	3
A's	2	1	5	4	4	T4	T3	3	1	1	1	4	2.75	4
Angels	6	5	1	T5	T2	2	1	T6	4	3	4	7	3.83	2
Chisox	5	4	3	1	T5	3	5	5	5	7	2	2	3.92	1
Twins	3	7	7	T5	T2	T4	6	1	2	5	7	1	4.17	2
Rangers	4	3	6	3	7	7	2	T6	6	4	3	3	4.50	0
Mariners	7	6	4	7	T5	6	7	4	7	6	5	5	5.75	0
EAST														
Tigers	5	4	4	2	1	3	3	1	2	7	3	2	3.08	2
Blue Jays	7	7	T6	4	2	1	4	2	T3	1	2	1	3.33	3
Bosox	4	5	3	6	4	5	1	5	1	3	1	2	3.33	3
Yankees	1	1	5	3	3	2	2	4	5	5	7	5	3.58	2
Brewers	3	2	1	5	7	6	6	3	T3	4	6	4	4.17	1
Orioles	2	3	2	1	5	4	7	6	7	2	5	6	4.17	1
Indians	6	6	T6	7	6	7	5	7	6	6	4	7	6.08	0

* Strike season—The division playoff winner is ranked first, its playoff opponent is second, and, if distinct, the team winning the most games for the season (e.g., the Reds) is listed third.
NOTE: T indicates a tie finish with another team.

period. With their first winning season ever in 1991, the Mariners may be showing some signs of life. The Indians are trying yet another youth movement, and, as with the Atlanta Braves, one of them will eventually take.

The caste system has been replaced by a dynamic market that is less predictable and far more exciting. The changes in the business of baseball are the clear cause of this new competitiveness. The enormous flow of revenue, the turnover on rosters, and the fans' insistence on a winner make for a lot more action from the front office.

The 1991 season offered striking evidence of the ties between the new business climate and competitiveness on the field, as the Minnesota Twins and the Atlanta Braves jumped from last to first in a single season, an unprecedented step. Both clubs had talented young players who were not quite ready for the majors in 1990, but the judicious use of free agency in picking up Jack Morris and Terry Pendleton, respectively, gave those young clubs some invaluable stability and experience for the pennant race.

The baseball of the 1950s may have been better in some respects than the game that is played now. The minor league apprenticeship was usually longer and more thorough, and other sports such as basketball and football were less likely to attract the top athletes in school. But if the game of our youth was better in some ways, it certainly was not so promising in the springtime for as many teams as it is today.

The predictable finishes of the postwar era were symptomatic of the business culture of the time. Like the antebellum South, much of postwar baseball was a society of fixed classes, defined roles, and little tolerance for dissenting views. And many of the franchises of that day were no more suited than Tara for the modern world.

The revolution in baseball is like many other revolutions because it concerns money and power; and it was well under way while the old order remained superficially unshaken.

From 1946 through 1957, while the major leagues integrated, moved a few franchises, and experimented with television, few saw how profoundly baseball was changing. The frontal attacks on the game's business structure were easily rebuffed, so the game's rulers basked in a false security.

Before Jackie Robinson's debut in Ebbets Field, the monopoly of the major leagues was challenged by the Pasquel brothers, who tried to improve Mexican baseball by making offers to some of the best major league players of the day, including Stan Musial. Their money was tempting enough to attract a few regulars, but neither Musial nor any other superstar took the risk.

The players who crossed the Rio Grande returned after a couple of seasons to a vindictive reaction from the major league owners and Commissioner Happy Chandler. The players were slapped with five-year suspensions—a penalty sufficient to ruin what was left of their career.

Danny Gardella and a few others sued in court to win immediate reinstatement. That plea was rejected, and the length of a formal trial on the merits threatened to add significant legal expenses to their suspensions.

Chandler then lifted his penalty, allowing the players to resume their careers. In his own account of the episode, the commissioner claimed that he was "tempering justice with mercy."[1] He had earlier allowed that "the Pasquel brothers were totally outlaw operators, and were not at all interested in what was decent and beneficial for the major leagues in the United States."[2]

What a remarkable perspective, that Mexican baseball officials should be concerned about the major league game. The Pasquels saw players who were underpaid and saw an opportunity to improve their own league by offering these men more money. Ban Johnson had done much the same thing when he established the American League. The Pasquels proved to be inept at sustaining their plan, but the idea itself was simple free enterprise.

In his memoir, Chandler also wrote about another "major

crisis of 1946"—a plan to unionize major league players was proposed by the Pittsburgh Pirates.[3] Chandler acknowledged that the players had some grievances, "but no strike! Any player who walked out I would immediately suspend from organized baseball."[4]

Like the Pasquel brothers, the players were proposing that the business of baseball operate on the principals of a market and that the players enjoy the right of any other American worker to organize and bargain collectively. The shock that these ideas had on baseball's rulers speaks volumes about the business culture of the time.

Baseball's feudal structure remained intact through the 1950s. It withstood a suit by George Toolson, a New York Yankee who balked at being sent down to the Binghamton farm team. His unsuccessful argument that the reserve clause constituted a restraint of trade directly challenged the 1922 Supreme Court decision that exempted baseball from antitrust law.

The major league owners rebuffed these attempts to change the nature of labor relations in baseball, and they also repelled potential competition from a powerful minor league. The Pacific Coast League tried to become a third major league after World War II. The majors succeeded in stalling and undermining the effort, and the monopoly of the American and National leagues was preserved.

House and Senate hearings reviewed baseball's antitrust exemption in the 1950s but declined to alter the legal anomaly. From all appearances, the owners were secure in their fiefdoms. In the postwar era, they faced rebellions from players, foreign owners, and minor leagues, and they crushed each challenge.

From our perspective, we can see that the old order of baseball was collapsing despite these superficial victories. The Lords of Baseball, in Harold Parrott's apt phrase, were about to be pulled from their thrones, and the great baseball families would abandon their estates like bankrupt royalty leaving the castle to the tourists.

Some of those families successfully adjusted to the first shocks of the postwar years. Tom Yawkey acquired the Red Sox in 1933, and he retained control until his death in 1978. His widow remained a partner, but the family is no longer directly involved in the running of the club.

Philip Wrigley bought the Chicago Cubs in 1925, and he passed the franchise on to his son and namesake a few years later. The family chewing gum fortune allowed the Cubs to be run as a kind of hobby while the team lagged near the bottom of the National League. Yet the Wrigleys kept the ownership until 1981, when they sold the Cubs to the Tribune Company.

The Giants were purchased by Charles Stoneham after World War I, and he gave the team to his son Horace in 1936. Horace ran the club with something less than strict sobriety, and he managed to lose money in New York in the 1950s despite the presence of Willie Mays in his prime. The move to San Francisco revived the franchise for a few more years, but the Stonehams were out of baseball in 1976.

Clark Griffith passed the Washington Senators to his nephew, Calvin, who moved the club to Minneapolis–St. Paul in 1961. Like Stoneham, Griffith held on for a while but sold the Twins when he was unable or unwilling to pay competitive salaries. Unlike Stoneham and Yawkey, the Griffiths treated baseball as a serious business in which revenues and expenses were centrally important items.

Those families spanned baseball generations from the emergence of Babe Ruth to the retirement of Willie Mays, but other families were less successful in the postwar period. Comiskey and Mack were names that in the nineteenth century were associated with player revolts and the upstart American League. By the 1950s, those names were tied to marginal franchises that were poorly prepared for the new challenges and opportunities of the day.

Charlie Comiskey's heirs were forced to sell the White Sox

to Bill Veeck before the Sox took the American League pennant in 1959, their first flag since the infamous 1919 season. Connie Mack remained with the Athletics into his nineties. The club foundered to a point at which he had to sell, and the new owner, Arnold Johnson, moved the club to Kansas City.

Walter Briggs was another of the owners who bought their clubs after World War I, but his wish to bequeath the Detroit Tigers to his son was blocked by family attorneys who stripped the franchise from the estate in 1954.

While the old families passed from the game, a few new ones entered for a time. Robert Carpenter picked up the Phillies for a song in 1943. He and his son kept the team long enough to have a World Series winner in 1980, then they sold the club in October 1981. John Galbreath bought the Pittsburgh Pirates in 1946, and his family retained the club into the 1980s, winning several championships during its tenure.

The most significant of the new family owners are the O'Malleys and the Busches. Walter O'Malley took controlling interest in the Brooklyn Dodgers from Branch Rickey in 1950, moved the team to Los Angeles after the 1957 season, and developed one of the top franchises in baseball. His son, Peter, succeeded in 1970 and remains one of the few full-time owners in the game today.

August Busch, Jr., purchased the St. Louis Cardinals in 1953 as a bauble to go with his principal business, the Anheuser-Busch breweries. The Cardinals are a team that is nominally owned by the Busch family, but the club has been run lately by Fred Kuhlman, a former executive of Anheuser-Busch.

Not every club in the postwar period was a family business. The Yankees were owned by Dan Topping and Del Webb, who purchased the club from the estate of Jacob Ruppert in 1948. Topping stayed with the Yankees through their greatest era, ending in 1964. He sold the club to the Columbia Broadcasting System, which held the Yankees during a decade of terrible clubs before the network sold the franchise to George Steinbrenner.

10

The most famous or notorious owner during the postwar years was Bill Veeck. He owned the Cleveland Indians and the St. Louis Browns, and owned the Chicago White Sox twice. Veeck was long on promotional schemes and short on cash. He integrated the American League and set attendance records in Cleveland. He forced the first franchise shifts when he owned the Browns. And he won a most improbable pennant with the White Sox in 1959. His last attempt at major league ownership ended with the Seitz ruling that inaugurated free agency in 1973. Veeck saw that baseball was about to enter a financial level that was beyond his means.

These owners comprised a fraternity of colleagues more than competitors. They cooperated to keep themselves ensconced in power, impervious to the complaints of players, fans, minor leagues, umpires, or any other underling. Although any of these owners would have been delighted with a championship, few were eager to rock the boat of racial bigotry to hire the players who could lead teams to a pennant. And virtually none of the owners was willing to relax the reserve clause, which would open the labor pool and foster greater competition.

The revolution in baseball took aim precisely at the comfort and complacency of the game's old order. Leisure and recreation for a prospering middle class grew more important in the postwar prosperity of America. Baseball needed to find the best players to attract fans, and that need drove up the costs of scouting and player development. Signing bonuses, higher travel costs to the new markets, and costly maintenance for aging ball parks added to the challenge of running a modern franchise. To cover these expenses, the teams had to draw more fans or secure lucrative broadcast contracts. All those new requirements meant that baseball operations would be more costly and complicated.

Over several decades, the small family operation that could stand marginal losses was becoming an outdated institution in baseball. Losses became intolerable because the investments in running the club had grown so significantly. Like a craps

11

game with higher stakes, the nickel-and-dime players were driven out by the high rollers.

The baseball front office that once operated with an owner and a general manager supported by some clerical help now required specialists. Ticket sales, scouting, community relations, marketing, stadium operations, publicity, and media relations are functions that today are distinct departments within most ball clubs. Baseball became one more industry in which the complexities of modern management made the old family store obsolete.

The complications of modern commerce may tempt fans to think of baseball today in terms of a dreary litany of legal and economic strife. We might compare the wonderful memories of the postwar years with a recitation that includes:

- strikes and lockouts;
- drug suspensions;
- arbitration battles;
- the Pete Rose affair;
- Steinbrenner's removal;
- and the specter of pay TV.

The comparison of the game of baseball in the 1950s with the business of baseball in the 1990s is off the mark. The memories of Williams, Musial, the New York game, and the other wonderful moments of our youth should make us appreciate the beauty of the game that is before us every day:

- Cal Ripken's streak;
- Cecil Fielder's magnificent return from Japan;
- Robin Yount on the way to 3,000 hits;
- Doc Gooden maybe on the way to 300 wins;
- Nolan Ryan's no-hitters;
- Rickey Henderson's stolen bases;
- and the swings of Darryl Strawberry and Will Clark.

The familiar lament that "it used to be a game but now it's a business" misses the point. Baseball was always a business, and in many ways it is a healthier one now. If we have to compare the present with the past (and as fans that exercise is inevitable), we should compare the game with the game and the business with the business. The game has changed since the 1950s, but it is at least as captivating as it was then—the attendance and broadcast figures bear that out.

The turmoil that we see is from the changes in the business of baseball. No longer do the owners keep a tight lid on their frustrated underlings. The old order is passing, and the transition is neither entirely smooth nor quiet. The business structure that will follow the despotism of sixteen major league owners is not entirely clear. The battles among lawyers and accountants that invade our sports pages reflect this stumbling search to settle a number of contentious issues. No matter how tedious some of these disputes can be, we can be hopeful, if not optimistic, that they may result in baseball being a stronger and healthier institution.

To start to appreciate the baseball of this modern corporate era, we should remember that the baseball of our memory was provincially limited in several important respects—an all-white game of sixteen major league teams confined to ten cities in the northeast quadrant of the country. To accommodate the nation that America would become, baseball had to change. It had to drop the contrived barriers of its past, like racism, and adapt to new technology, like jet air travel, that would carry the game to every section of the country.

These changes have occurred in fits and starts, making baseball today often seem all chaos and controversy, but that is as misleading as our postwar nostalgia. Some patterns are becoming clearer, and they suggest that baseball may be entering an era of spectacular success.

The major leagues have not only broken out of the northeast United States, but they have left the United States to establish the Toronto Blue Jays and the Montreal Expos, international outposts of major league franchises. The search for players has gone far beyond North America. The Dominican Republic is the most familiar source of foreign talent, but the roots of an international game are beginning to flourish all over the world.

Several major league teams have training facilities in Australia with players on their way to the majors. Camps have opened in China. Taiwan has its first professional team—something for those brilliant, driven Little Leaguers to dream about. As an Olympic sport, baseball will develop players throughout Europe, Russia and, conceivably, Africa. All of that would build on the game's traditional base in Japan and Latin America. How long will it be before the major leagues include dozens of foreign-born players from Europe and Asia? How long before a true World Series pits the winners of continental championships?

Baseball broadcasts rest on elaborate contractual agreements between the major leagues and television networks. But technology suggests that fans may soon be able to see the games that *they* want, not the games that baseball officials and network executives decide to send them. Despite current economic and legal fulminations, a future fan may for a modest amount of money pick the game of one's choice from a satellite. Baseball will no longer be bound by geography.

In the near future, fans will not just passively watch games. With the aid of computers, microcameras, and high-definition television, fans will select the camera angle that they prefer, compete with other fans to guess how a particular player will perform, and buy tickets by punching a few buttons on a keyboard. "Consumer sovereignty" will be more than the rhetoric of free-market economists.

Architects are rediscovering baseball's geometry. The next generation of stadiums has arrived, and it is a great improvement over the last. The benefits of the neighborhood park are being combined with the conveniences of the modern stadiums. Renewed attention to maintaining clean, safe facilities that will attract families is a hallmark of most stadium operations now.

*   *   *

The challenge that could frustrate baseball's golden future concerns the sharing of the sport's riches. Presently, baseball's prosperity is abundant but unbalanced. The purported advantages of large-market teams over those in smaller communities is frequently discussed, but that is only one potential problem.

Some franchises were purchased years ago and are now owned free and clear. Those owners have a considerable advantage over their colleagues who may have paid nearly $100 million for a club and have significant loan repayments on top of salaries and other operational expenses.

Clubs with favorable stadium leases and those few that own their facilities are in a better position than franchises that struggle with an unappealing park in a bad part of town. But in the great stadium game, our concern should be reserved for the community that negotiates with club operators over a new ball park. The record shows that when franchises and cities talk about new stadiums, the public purse is in some jeopardy.

Expansion recalls the old saw about appointments to public office: the exercise creates enemies and ingrates. The disappointed suitors may turn their charms on established clubs that have become disgruntled in their familiar markets. If an older club relocates, a cycle may begin in which abandoned cities press for further expansion accompanied with the threat of an antitrust suit.

The new wonders of broadcasting will be a far cry from black-and-white network broadcasts with Dizzy Dean presiding. The potential wrinkle is the price. Providing games on "free" television may become obsolete, and some people will not be able to afford the new technology. The loss of a familiar and beloved entertainment raises issues in political settings in which baseball is still seen as a right that the public is entitled to enjoy more than a product that it may choose to purchase.

The sad episodes of drug and alcohol abuse expose the human frailties of some of our heroes. Otis Nixon and Steve Howe have shown that the drug problem persists, and baseball faces a serious problem with its relationship to alcohol.

THE DIAMOND REVOLUTION

Severing the tie to beer would be the single step that could collapse the economic structure of baseball. How the public sorts out its attitude about drinking will be critical to the financial future of baseball.

The labor climate probably has aggravated more fans than any other issue. The merits of the players' and owners' arguments may be sound, but their economic theories are uninteresting to many fans who see simply a battle among millionaires about how to carve a pie that is far larger than anyone could have imagined.

The commercial contention that can be such a distraction from the game we love may just be growing pains before the game assumes an international scope. The period since World War II has established two points: that baseball can be an enormously profitable enterprise and that the old feudal structure of that business is thoroughly inadequate to our times. But what will follow?

The way that baseball develops its opportunities will be shaped to a great extent by the way that it understands its recent past. The revolution in baseball has been progressing for decades, and it has many years to go before it will be complete. The glorious new era that awaits could easily be scuttled by choices dictated by fear and suspicion. But if the right lessons are learned from that recent history, then the future will likely find baseball bringing the excitement to the entire world that it has brought to this country for more than a century.

NOTES

1. Happy Chandler, *Heros, Plain Folks, and Skunks: The Life and Times of Happy Chandler* (Chicago: Bonus Books, 1959), p. 185.
2. Ibid, p. 183.
3. Ibid, p. 190.
4. Ibid, p. 191.

2

Beyond the Plantation Game

Baseball's history of racial bigotry dispels two of the great myths on which the game relies. In the culture of sports, we are taught that every effort consistent with sportsmanship must be spent to achieve victory. Players like Pete Rose and managers like Earl Weaver may not be universally beloved, but they have been generally respected because of their dedication to winning.

Similarly, in the culture of business, we learn that prosperity and profits must be pursued with a steady gaze, indifferent to emotional impulses that could distract us from the balance sheet. Some economists assure us that human behavior is rational in making the decisions that maximize our gains and minimize our losses. But the ban against black players that began to fall in 1947, and the prejudices that have since persisted, belie those assurances.

The myths of sports and business both teach that competition forces us to perform our best. We run faster, leap higher, and make better widgets because if we do not, someone else will win the prize or the market share. Cooperation is fine to a point—we sometimes need to work with others to maximize our efforts—but in the end, the competitive drive to win is the foundation of progress in our culture and our economy.

THE DIAMOND REVOLUTION

Baseball happily admits to having its colorful eccentrics both on the field and in the front offices, but it presents even these characters in context: Casey Stengel, Charlie Finley, and all their kindred souls may have always been good for a story, but ultimately they were just trying to win and make a dollar.

The myths are so powerful that the meaning of baseball's color barrier is slow to be grasped, but it was simply a preference for the comfort of shared prejudice over the rigors of competition. Before integration—and even for some years after it—general managers worked relentlessly to find one or two players who might improve their ball clubs. Scouts were sent to the most remote hamlets to verify rumors about a prospect. Money was invested in farm systems to nurture players for the big leagues. Coaches worked for hours on end to hone the skills of marginal major leaguers. Meanwhile, under the noses of the major league owners were dozens of the best players who ever lived, and they were available for the asking.

The injustice to black players who were deprived of major league opportunities is obvious and well documented.[1] Perhaps less obvious is the damage to the game and to specific teams who deprived themselves of improvement by their bigotry.

This self-inflicted damage is one of the features about racial discrimination that Martin Luther King, Jr., among others, addressed. In banishing or subjugating another group of people, we inevitably deprive ourselves of their talents, and we turn ourselves into bestial oppressors. We dismiss the harm we do to the objects of this persecution by stigmatizing them as somehow less than us. We can further ignore the damage that we cause ourselves by casting our history in a false light of folklore that diverts attention away from the abusive practice.

The so-called Golden Age of Sports in the 1920s, for example, certainly included its heroic figures. But using the very standard of competition that our myths revere, the achievements of Babe Ruth, golfer Bobby Jones, and tennis great Bill Tilden are tainted because the competition was racially rigged. This delusion has especially affected our understanding of our national game.

The early years of baseball in this century are recalled as a rough game with no quarter given or expected, but in limiting itself to white players the game was seriously diminished. Ty Cobb, for example, retains the reputation of a fierce, even dirty competitor who would do anything to win. From 1905 through 1928, Cobb played on three pennant winners, the Detroit Tigers of 1907–9. He spent the bulk of his career chasing Connie Mack's Athletics and Babe Ruth's Yankees. His brilliant individual career never turned the Tigers into a dynasty, for even the pennant winners never won a World Series.

Given his reputation, Cobb must have been excruciatingly frustrated as the Tigers spent most of his career in the middle of the pack, rarely in a pennant race in September. The mythology of sports would lead us to think that Cobb must have been desperate to find some way for the Tigers to break out of their mediocrity, but the mythology would obscure the obvious and available solution to Cobb's frustration.

Oscar Charleton, Smokey Joe Williams, Bullet Rogan, Jose Mendez, and other contemporaries almost certainly would have made a decisive difference in the Tigers' fortunes, but Cobb would not recommend the signing of the great black players he saw in barnstorming games. He appears to have been secure with the white supremacist attitudes that marked his native Georgia during his boyhood in the period after Reconstruction.

Another advocate of the rough, win-at-all-costs style of baseball that was played early in the century was John Mc-Graw. He at least saw the possibilities of what black players could do for baseball. In 1901, he even tried to portray Frank Grant, a black man, as Charlie Tokohama, a Cherokee, but the ploy failed. Thereafter, McGraw meekly complied with the custom that barred black players. He never hesitated to challenge the umpires and league executives when his club's interests were at stake, but he backed down on this issue. As passionately as McGraw wanted to win, he acceded to the racial bigotry of his time.

Cobb, McGraw, and other players and managers were relatively powerless at that time in baseball's history. The owners had the means to change baseball's racial configuration if they had wanted, but they proved blind to their own interest in winning and making money. Connie Mack had a more gentlemanly demeanor than did either Cobb or McGraw, but he was just as determined to win. From 1901 to 1950, Mack led a Philadelphia Athletics franchise that was generally either a dynasty or a doormat.

For its first fifteen years, the club was one of the powers of the American League, winning six pennants and three world championships. When the Federal League organized in 1914, Mack was faced with paying his players fair market salaries, and the prospect was too much for him. He sold off his stars, and the Athletics finished in the cellar for the next seven years.

The team became competitive again in 1925, as it battled the Yankees. Mack ended the Ruthian era with three consecutive pennants from 1929 to 1931. Those clubs won 104, 102, and 107 games, respectively, along with two more world championships. The Athletics remained a strong team until 1934, when they slid to a fifth-place finish. Ten more years in last place were ahead for Mack.

Connie Mack was one of the great executives in baseball history. He assembled some of the best teams that have ever played, and he stayed with the game during lean years. His refusal to pay fair salaries to keep great players seems eccentric, but even more bizarre was his patience during the years of futility, when a few black players would have reversed the Athletics' fortunes.

Mack was aware of the great players in the Negro leagues,

and he knew Rube Foster, the impresario of black baseball at that time. During the 1929 World Series, when the Athletics were short of players, Mack may have considered signing some black stars to bolster his roster. Robert Peterson relates that story in his book *Only the Ball Was White* and he concludes that Mack refrained because he was intimidated by the other owners.[2]

In his later years, Mack was asked by Judy Johnson, the black former star whom Mack had hired as a scout, why he had not hired black players. Mack replied that there were so many capable blacks that too many white players would have lost their jobs. Apparently, he did not explain why that would have been a problem, because white men routinely lost their jobs to better white players—just what our economic mythology celebrates.

The color barrier becomes especially puzzling when its effects on competition are considered. While Griffith, Briggs, Stoneham, Comiskey, and the rest of the old guard were occasionally putting terrific teams on the field, the New York Yankees were developing something unique in baseball.

The Yankees were not simply a great team—the game had produced a number of great teams—the Yankees became a great organization that routinely produced great teams. The Boys of Summer and the Big Red Machine were tremendous teams for five to seven years, but the Yankees dominated baseball from 1920 to the mid-1960s.

Signing black players was the obvious move to challenge the Yankees dynasty, yet no organization seriously considered the step. Men who devoted their professional life to winning, to beating their competition, to doing their best, to making money, routinely abandoned these goals to preserve the racist ban.

One example of this self-defeating bigotry was the Pittsburgh Pirates, who were a long time recovering from being swept in the 1927 World Series. The Bucs would not win another pennant until 1960, but they came close several times during the 1930s. They finished four games behind the Cubs in 1932, five back of the Giants in 1933, and two behind the Cubs again in 1938.

Those three pennant runs were made with rather thin pitching. Larry French was the Pirates ace in the early 1930s, and although he won 197 games in his career, he was dealt to the Cubs in 1934 after six seasons with Pittsburgh. None of the other Pirates pitchers of that era are particularly memorable. The team had a terrific offense, powered by the Waner brothers and Arky Vaughan. A couple of great pitchers might have made the club a dynasty.

The pitchers were available. Satchel Paige was only the most famous. Bullet Rogan was still pitching effectively during the 1930s; Ted Trent is said to have struck out Bill Terry four times in an exhibition game; Slim Jones and Bill Jackman are two other great pitchers of that period whom author Robert Peterson cites as outstanding performers in the Negro League.

Perhaps none of these pitchers would have brought a championship to Pittsburgh, but they certainly deserved a look. The problem with the Pirates pitching staff during the 1930s was not the scarcity of talent but the refusal by the Pirates front office to sign the available talent. The executives' failure to see that Paige and Rogan might have brought glory to Forbes Field fatally limited the opportunities for the Pirates on the diamond.

The most egregious blunder by the Pirates brass during the 1930s was their inept pursuit of a catcher. Several men held the position for a few years, but none of them added much to the Pirates attack. In another part of town, playing for the Homestead Grays, was one of the great catchers of all time.

Josh Gibson could have been for the Pirates what Yogi Berra, Roy Campanella, and Johnny Bench were for their clubs—tremendous power hitters who were league MVPs. Any fair-minded person could quickly see what an injustice the color barrier was to Gibson, but what should also be appreciated is how destructive it was to the Pirates.

Beyond the Plantation Game

The Pirates were just one club that might have been dramatically better with a few black players. The Boston Red Sox were another team that sacrificed winning for bigotry. Consider their record during the 1930s:

Boston Red Sox Finishes in the 1930s

YEAR	RECORD	FINISH	GAMES BEHIND	PENNANT WINNER
1930	52–102	8th	50	Philadelphia
1931	62–90	6th	45	Philadelphia
1932	43–111	8th	64	New York
1933	63–86	7th	34.5	Washington
1934	76–76	4th	24	Detroit
1935	78–75	4th	16	Detroit
1936	74–80	6th	28.5	New York
1937	80–72	5th	21	New York
1938	88–61	2nd	9.5	New York
1939	89–62	2nd	17	New York

Tom Yawkey's purchase of the club in 1933 brought the Sox back to a respectable level, and the arrivals of Jimmie Foxx in 1936, Bobby Doerr in 1937, and Ted Williams in 1939 improved the team significantly. They needed still more help to close on the Yankees of Joe DiMaggio, yet the front office passed up the players who might have rewritten the history of American League baseball.

Baseball's mythology casts a glow on the memory of Tom Yawkey that preserves him as a benevolent sportsman who was generous to his players, yet few would deny that Yawkey's racial attitudes were similar to Ty Cobb's. Cobb's racism was obscured behind his vicious determination, and Yawkey's was subsumed beneath his kindly demeanor. Both men are remembered for their intense eagerness to win, yet Cobb's other vices and Yawkey's virtues can distract us from the fact that their bigotry was the common overriding reason why neither won the World Series title that each desperately wanted.

23

THE DIAMOND REVOLUTION

For much of their history, the Red Sox have traded on a romantic mystique that the club is doomed. The "curse of Harry Frazee," who sold Babe Ruth to the Yankees, is said to have kept the great Bosox teams from championships. The few pennants have resulted only in frustrating World Series defeats.

The charms of rooting for the Red Sox have captivated some of baseball's most gifted apologists, including Bart Giamatti. The intellectuals invoke muses, angels, and perhaps the Devil to explain the ghosts that haunt Fenway. But the simple truth of much of the team's misfortune is more profane: at least until the 1960s, championships eluded the Red Sox because they were committed to bigoted management.

Red Sox officials watched while Jackie Robinson, Henry Aaron, Willie Mays, and other black stars took their teams to another level. The Red Sox chased the Yankees through the 1940s and 1950s with a strong team that had some glaring deficiencies that black players could have filled. They came up short not because they were doomed, but because they were blind to their own interests. During those years, the Red Sox suffered far less from fate than from their front office.

The Brooklyn Dodgers have been assigned a somewhat heroic place in baseball history as the team that finally broke the color barrier, but the record of that franchise makes clear that the Dodgers were another organization that should have felt compelled to integrate long before it did. After their pennant-winning season in 1920, the Dodgers struggled until 1941 before capturing another championship. They finished a game and a half back from the Giants in 1924, but they spent two decades trying to avert bankruptcy while the Giants contended for National League titles and the Yankees became a metaphor for excellence.

It should have been natural for the Dodgers to take the democratic step of dropping the color barrier back in the 1920s. The Yankees were the darlings of New York society, and the Giants were well-heeled foes ensconced across the

Harlem River in the Polo Grounds. The Dodgers did not beat the Giants in attendance until 1930, and the Bums trailed both the Giants and the Yankees at the gate thirty-one times during the years 1903–38. The team of the unappreciated borough of Brooklyn would never be followed by New York's swells, so why not pursue money and championships by taking the dramatic step of hiring great black players to leapfrog the competition?

The Cubs, Braves, White Sox, Indians, and Tigers are some of the other clubs in northern markets that should have seen how integration would have benefited them. In fact, the only club that profited from the racist ban was the Yankees, who won while other teams settled for second best in all-white comfort.

Since the myths of competition and winning that govern sports and business were belied by the color barrier, what explains the complacency of teams who lost games and money under the code of racism? One serious obstacle to any owner who might have wished to sign a black player was Commissioner Kenesaw Mountain Landis. In his autobiography, *Veeck as in Wreck*, Bill Veeck writes that he paid a courtesy call on Landis in 1943 to relate his plans to buy the bankrupt Philadelphia Phillies and sign a number of black stars.[3] Before Veeck could close the deal, the Phillies were sold to William Cox, apparently because Landis was unalterably opposed to integrating baseball. But singling out Landis as the reason why the color barrier persisted is no more sufficient than singling out Cap Anson as the sole reason why the ban was imposed in the first place. Landis had many strong opinions, including his fierce opposition to the development of farm systems, but clubs persisted in buying minor league teams because they saw economic advantages to doing so. Similar advantages would have accrued to a club that would have been willing to defy Landis on racial integration.

Landis's passing did not release a pent-up enthusiasm for

signing black players. When Branch Rickey proposed bringing Robinson to the Dodgers in 1947, he was opposed in a poll of the other clubs by a 15–1 vote. The reluctance to sign black players persisted long after Landis's death and long after Jackie Robinson exposed the folly of the color barrier in his rookie season. While the Cleveland Indians, under Bill Veeck's ownership, and the St. Louis Browns both put black men on the field in July 1947, no other club followed suit until 1949 when the Giants brought up Hank Thompson and Monte Irvin.[4] Sam Jethroe broke the barrier for the Braves in 1950, and the White Sox traded for Minnie Minoso in 1951.

Five years after the color barrier was first broken, most of the major league clubs had never played a black man, and the 1952 season passed without any more progress. The impressive records that Robinson, Irvin, Mays, Campanella, and Don Newcombe had already established were less influential on the owners than the traditional and irrational attitude of the fraternity that no blacks need apply.

When the major league rosters expanded in September 1953, the Cubs brought up Ernie Banks and the Athletics signed their first black player. The 1954 season saw additional progress as the Pirates, Cardinals, Reds, and Yankees integrated in the spring, and the Senators came on board in September.

The diehards included the Phillies, who finally brought up John Kennedy for a cup of coffee in April 1957 to complete the integration of the National League. The Detroit Tigers picked up Ozzie Virgil from the Giants in June 1958, and the Red Sox ended their holdout by signing Pumpsie Green, who appeared in Fenway in July 1959.

By 1950, Commissioner Landis was out of the picture, and the ability of blacks to compete was established, yet most teams were reluctant to integrate. Why?

One of the fears that must have troubled the owners was the concern that fans would not pay to see a black player. What would have happened if the game had integrated years earlier is inevitably speculative, but the results from the 1950s show that those fears were unwarranted.

Team Attendance and Finish Before and After Integration[5]

TEAM	YEAR BEFORE INTEGRATION			YEAR OF INTEGRATION*		
NL						
Dodgers	1946	1,796,824	T1st	1947	1,807,526	1st
Giants	1948	1,459,269	5th	1949	1,218,446	5th
Braves	1949	1,081,795	4th	1950	944,391	4th
Cardinals	1953	880,242	3rd	1954	1,146,230	6th
Cubs	1953	763,658	7th	1954	748,183	7th
Pirates	1953	572,757	8th	1954	475,494	8th
Reds	1953	548,063	6th	1954	704,167	5th
Phillies	1956	934,798	5th	1957	1,146,230	5th
AL						
Indians	1946	1,057,289	6th	1947	1,521,978	4th
Browns	1946	526,435	7th	1947	320,474	8th
White Sox	1950	781,330	6th	1951	1,328,234	4th
Athletics	1953	362,113	7th	1954	304,666	8th
Yankees	1953	1,537,811	1st	1954	1,475,171	2nd
Senators	1954	503,542	6th	1955	425,238	8th
Tigers	1957	1,272,346	4th	1958	1,098,924	5th
Red Sox	1958	1,077,047	3rd	1959	984,102	5th

* If the player came up in September, the following year is counted as the first year of integration.

In the National League, the attendance for four teams increased, while for four teams it declined. The finishes for six teams remained identical, improved for one club, and dropped for the other.

American League fans were similarly more affected by a club's performance than by skin color. Six teams saw their attendances drop, while two improved. But those six also finished lower the next year, while the remaining two clubs moved up in the standings.

A few of the figures are intriguing. The Browns' experiment

to boost the crowds in 1947 through integration was a complete bust—a 40% drop. But in that same town where Jim Crow reigned in Sportsman's Park, the Cardinals' attendance jumped 30% when they integrated a few years later.

In Boston, the teams followed very different strategies with nearly identical results. The Braves were one of the first teams to play a black man, and their attendance fell by 137,404. Nearly a decade later, the Red Sox attendance in their last all-white season was within five thousand of what the Braves had drawn in 1949. The Bosox crowds slid the following year by 92,945.

The Indians' attendance jumped 50% during their first year, and they were the first club in the majors to top 2 million the year after that. But they were also improving significantly in the standings, and their attendance dropped in later years when their performance fell.

Perhaps before World War II, the integration of baseball would have provoked riots and boycotts, but the evidence from the 1950s suggests that fans are more interested in good baseball than in prejudices that weaken the game.

As the owners opened their minds to the prospect of hiring black players, both the sport and business of baseball were historically affected. First, the game improved dramatically for an obvious reason. Professional baseball is played by men who with few exceptions are between the ages of twenty and forty. In 1950, the population of white males in America in their twenties and thirties was 20,449,808.[6] By opening the game to black men in that same age-group, the number of potential ballplayers increased by 2,184,790. A more than 10% growth in the eligible labor pool is especially significant because the rosters of major league clubs in 1950 totaled only 400 players.

Even with the dilatory hiring practices of many teams, black players by the end of the 1950s had established beyond doubt that the game that preceded their arrival was an inferior product. Since the integration of baseball in 1947, the superstar strata among players has been disproportionately dominated by black men. Despite the slow pace of integration during the 1950s, the principal offensive categories have been led by a black player an incredible number of times during that forty-four-season span.

Offensive Championships Won by Black Players,
1947–90 (44 years)

	NATIONAL LEAGUE	AMERICAN LEAGUE
Batting	28	14
Home Run	20	15
RBI	23	15
Runs Scored	22	15
Stolen Bases	41	27

To see that blacks have won about half the hitting and power titles in the National League and about one-third in the American League is enough to dispel any doubts about what they have brought to the game. But the numbers do not adequately convey how the addition of speed that Jackie Robinson reintroduced and that Maury Wills, Lou Brock, and Rickey Henderson have refined has transformed the game. Speed puts tremendous pressure on opposing pitchers and defenses. A walk is not just aggravating, it has become potentially decisive.

While the opportunities to become pitchers have been especially limited for black players, that prejudice seems also to be easing. The great seasons of Don Newcombe and Joe Black during the 1950s, the magnificent careers of Bob Gibson and Ferguson Jenkins, the drama of Vida Blue and Mike Norris in Oakland, and Doc Gooden's success in New York belie any doubts that blacks can perform at that position or that fans will pay to see them do so.

In the relatively brief time that blacks have been allowed in the major leagues, they have dominated not only the past forty years of baseball, but they have also established a remarkable record on the game's all-time lists. In the history of major league baseball, sixteen batters have accumulated 3,000 hits in their career; five of them are black. Thirty-two have driven in more than 1,500 runs, nine of them are black. Fourteen have hit more than 500 home runs; six of them are black. Since 1962, one-third of the inductees into the Hall of Fame have been players who would not have been allowed on the field before 1947.

When we think about how impoverished postwar baseball would have been without Willie Mays, Henry Aaron, Ernie Banks, Jackie Robinson, and Frank Robinson, we have to shudder at what was lost to five decades of racism. More than the spitball, Babe Ruth, day games, train travel, or any other person or quality, baseball before 1947 was characterized by racism. The great achievements of Cobb, Walter Johnson, Christy Mathewson, Lou Gehrig, and the other legends cannot rescue the era of bigotry from a tainted place in the game's history. Baseball certainly enjoyed great players and teams before 1947, but they were never tested as they might have been.

The gradual hiring of blacks by the major leagues during the 1950s settled an issue for baseball that would become contentious for the larger community. During the 1950s and 1960s, integration was the strategy of the mainstream civil rights movement in its pursuit of racial justice. The Reverend King, Robert Kennedy, and other leaders of the movement assumed that blacks could fit into American society much as European whites had. Prejudice would give way to assimilation as it had for the Irish, the Italians, and other immigrants. Each of these racial and ethnic groups would retain an identity that could be celebrated annually in some community parade, but that identification would cease to be a barrier to social and economic progress.

Beyond the Plantation Game

After many years of struggle, many frustrations, and too many martyrs, the civil rights movement had secured its great victories. The de jure segregation of the South had been effectively eliminated. Court decisions, new laws, and administrative enforcement largely eliminated the use of the law to separate and stigmatize African Americans.

Conditions had decidedly improved for blacks, and that progress was certainly evident in baseball. By the mid-1960s, black players were included among the best-paid and most respected men in the game. By any standard, Bob Gibson enjoyed a richer career than Satchel Paige. Ernie Banks was nationally famous where Oscar Charleton was unknown. Willie Mays was acclaimed where Cool Papa Bell remained relatively unappreciated.

The achievements in racial justice that had been a dream when Jackie Robinson broke in were undeniably significant, but they remained somewhat hollow. America's legal system had been formally cleansed of racial discrimination, but bigotry continued to plague the country. In the 1840s, Alexis de Tocqueville had predicted that color would confound America's race relations well after slavery itself had been abolished, and by the late 1960s it was depressingly clear how accurate Tocqueville's prediction had been.

The frustrations that exploded in Watts, Newark, and Detroit during the 1960s contributed to an alternative objective to the goal of integration. Some blacks began to promote the idea of separation on the belief that they would never be accepted by white society and would be in danger of losing the beauty of their African heritage if they continued trying to fit in.

Stokely Carmichael, H. Rap Brown, Huey Newton, and other young challengers to King's leadership repudiated the goals of integration and called for blacks to develop their own economy as a means of acquiring power. Although never widely acknowledged, baseball had provided a test of the competing strategies with results that remain somewhat ambiguous.

31

THE DIAMOND REVOLUTION

The principal source of black players for the major leagues were the Negro leagues that had been around since about 1920. These associations were slightly more stable than the barnstorming teams that carried disorganized baseball all across America. Many of the owners of the all-black teams were black businessmen whose income was derived from some of the shadier commercial pursuits.

The black franchises were financially marginal businesses, but they occasionally drew crowds to major league parks that eclipsed the typical day's attendance of the host team. During the 1930s, the Negro All-Star games could fill a park like Yankee Stadium with a market of fans that the major league owners continued to ignore.

With few exceptions, the major league owners refused to recognize the black clubs as legitimate businesses. After 1947, when a team in the National or American League found a prospect on a club like the Kansas City Monarchs, the player generally was signed to a major league contract with no compensation for the franchise that had found and developed him.

Some of the Negro League owners objected to the theft of their players. Effa Manley, who owned the Newark Eagles with her husband, Abe, was faced with the painful choice of promoting the integration of the major leagues at the price of her own business. Manley bitterly complained to Branch Rickey about some of his raids, but Rickey made clear that players would no longer be signed from teams in the Negro leagues if compensation were required.

As it happened, integration was the end of the Negro leagues. In the context of the civil rights movement, the loss of those teams was a small price for the victory of having great black players on the same field with white major leaguers. But from the later perspective of black separatists, the victory may not have been so worthwhile. White America had claimed the cream of black enterprise without respecting or seriously acknowledging how those players had gotten from small southern towns to the great ball parks of the North.

Mays, Aaron, and Banks were often acclaimed as "natural" athletes without regard for the organizations that had developed their skills. Some sportswriters and baseball executives, as well as the black players themselves, knew of the business talent that kept teams going despite a hostile climate, but that part of the story was lost in the celebration of integration.

The pattern was repeated a few years later when the fight for racial justice in baseball moved beyond the ball parks to the accommodations that teams were afforded. As hotels and restaurants dropped their own ban on black players, economic effects rippled through black communities.

Don Newcombe joined the Dodgers in 1949, and he compiled a distinguished record, including Rookie of the Year, Cy Young, and Most Valuable Player awards. Now the Dodgers director for community relations, Newcombe remembers hotels and restaurants that prospered by catering to black ballplayers.[7] Within the isolated black economy of a city like St. Louis, the hotel where Jackie stayed would have instant status. The favorite restaurant of Campanella or Aaron would draw patrons who wanted to dine where their favorite players ate.

Newcombe recalls that integration had a devastating effect on those ancillary black businesses. He displays some mixed feelings about having left those establishments when the all-white hotels finally saw the light of day. The years of resentment that one was not welcome in the best places in town left it effectively impossible for black players to reject the opportunity when it finally came.

Deprived of their most famous customers, many of those black businesses, Newcombe believes, did not survive integration. Segregation had brought a measure of prosperity to the black communities of the great cities of the 1950s, and critical resources may have been assimilated into white society when racial barriers toppled.

In Newcombe's face one can see a black man's ambiguity about racial progress. He knows that he had enjoyed rewards that Bullet Rogan never knew, but he also lived through years of hatred and bigotry when he was not welcome at places with his teammates. Clubs were slow to insist that all their players be treated as equals or business would be taken elsewhere. A special affection must remain for the businesses where Newcombe and other black men were welcomed, indeed lionized, in an otherwise hostile time.

The differing perspectives on race relations is also clear when Newcombe is asked about the end of racial harassment on the field. Did league officials finally demand an end to the abuses that Robinson endured in his first seasons? Did individual umpires inform benches that epithets would not be permitted that day? To Newcombe, those questions seem remarkably naive.

In fact, the harassment ceased as black players stood up for themselves and for one another. Newcombe remembers a game against the Phillies in 1950 during which vicious racial remarks were spewed from the Phillies dugout. After one particular outburst from a coach, Newcombe put the batter, Del Ennis, on his back with a fastball. Ennis called time, walked to the Phillies bench for a short conversation, then returned to bat. Silence ensued.

Years later, Newcombe reminded Ennis of the incident and asked the former outfielder what he had said to the coach. Ennis replied that he had told the coach to shut up or lose his tongue.

What Newcombe remembers is a very specific set of self-reliant actions by black players to overcome the bigotry that they faced on the field. Another star of that era recalls somewhat differently the development of tolerance among the players. Al Rosen offers an important perspective on the struggle for justice in baseball.[8] Rosen is a Jew who grew up in South Carolina, a witness to segregation, and an object of anti-Semitism.

The key factor in ending the most overt expressions of bigotry, according to Rosen, was the talent of the black players. Once people saw how good they were, he recalls, fans and other players appreciated them as athletes and the taunts abated.

Rosen acknowledges that some bigots were unchanged by anything they saw on the field, and because of that he believes that a league directive or demands for civility from umpires would have backfired. Rosen believes that prejudiced people tend not to respect authority, so an insistence on decency might not have had the desired effect.

The versions of history that Newcombe and Rosen remember may be more complementary than contradictory. Many white players and fans may have quickly welcomed the black players out of a sense of justice, an appreciation for their skills, an eagerness for the money they would bring to the team, or a combination of motives. Understandably, black players would remember the lingering bitterness and what they themselves had to do to correct the problem.

From the vantage of a black separatist, what the major leagues did during the 1950s was take for their own profit some of the best baseball players in the country. The black businesses that relied on those players were dismissed without a thought, and the players themselves were unprotected against abuse and social ostracism. The progress that was made came at a dear price, and the respect that the players earned was won by their own efforts. One need not be a black separatist to see that the racial progress in baseball during the 1950s might inspire reactions other than gratitude.

The integration of baseball was not only the single step that has most improved the game, it has also been a critical component in the radical changes in the business of baseball. The inclusion of blacks on major league rosters was a terribly important symbol of the struggle for racial justice, because some bigotry was relieved when people saw that men rather than stereotypes came to the plate.

At the same time that baseball made its most significant social contribution, another irony about this triumph of justice gradually became clear: the black players had been liberated to join a caste system. They were roughly as free and equal as the white players, which meant that they were not able to work where they wanted for the employer of their choice for a wage that had been determined in a competitive market. The comparisons between baseball's reserve clause and slavery were overly dramatic, but they understandably struck a chord among some of the black players.

During the 1960s, as the civil rights struggle moved beyond courtrooms and legislative chambers, a fresh militancy infused the movement with calls for Black Power—a bold expression of pride in the African heritage, an expression that seemed to thrive on making white people in authority uncomfortable.

Sports provided the most famous apostle of the new attitude, Muhammad Ali. He first bragged about his skill, his looks, and his future. He ridiculed his opponents with disparaging nicknames and predictions of knockout rounds. When he realized his boasts by taking the heavyweight title from Sonny Liston, he followed that shock with the equally remarkable announcement that Cassius Clay was no longer his name.

The Islamic name that he chose was part of his liberation from the cultures of slavery and Christianity. When Ali refused to accept induction into the armed forces because of his religious beliefs, the break with acceptable society and the established culture of sports was total. It would have been hard to imagine a personality more different from the last great black heavyweight champion, Joe Louis.

Boxing was probably the natural sport to express Black Power. No matter how maddening the rhetoric and behavior, Ali could not be ignored so long as he could pass the test of every playground in America: back up his talk with his fists.

Baseball was a different matter. Black Power found its way into some symbolic battles over the cut of stirrups on uniform socks, the expression of hyphenated expletives, and the hardy perennial of the 1960s and 1970s, hair. More serious, the forces of rebellion in black culture came to concentrate in baseball on the relationship between players and owners. Once the white leadership of the players union earned their trust, black players were the quickest to see the inherent flaws in their station, and they were the most eager to redress the injustice. As union chief Donald Fehr says of black players, "They understand who 'The Man' is."[9]

When Marvin Miller was hired in 1965 to pump some life into the players union, he found a rank and file that was infused with something less than the martial spirit.[10] Miller concludes that players had been brainwashed by owners and weak union leadership to believe that they were lucky to be paid anything to be playing a little boys' game.

Because Miller himself is white, he faced additional skepticism from black players as he tried to organize the union's challenge of the owners. Miller points to several important actions in winning the trust of black and Hispanic players. First, he spoke to the owners about the racial discrimination that persisted in the early 1970s in parts of Florida during spring training. The objections helped end some of the abuse of players that had continued in Florida's smaller towns.

Hispanic players began to receive copies of the collective bargaining agreement in Spanish. More important, Miller persuaded the owners to amend a restriction that limited Latin players to playing winter ball in their native countries. The ban prevented Cuban players from making any money over the winter, an important opportunity given the salaries of that time. After Miller's intervention, the Cubans were free to play for any club that wanted them. Miller recounts that although the effort was seemingly minor, nothing so simple ever yielded such gratitude.

At the same time, Alex Johnson was running afoul of front offices from coast to coast. From 1964 through 1976, Johnson played for eight clubs despite compiling a .288 lifetime batting average. Fights with teammates, the press, and club executives led to repeated reprimands and suspensions.

37

Johnson was hardly the first troubled player in baseball, but he was the first to be supported by the union. Miller recalls that it was apparent to him that Johnson was a young man who was emotionally troubled. Johnson's suspension was appealed, and he received treatment as well as back pay in the first case of a player going on the disabled list for an ailment other than physical injury.

None of these actions may now seem especially heroic, but at the time, no white man was taking these steps. In that context, black and Hispanic players saw that Miller was trustworthy, so when he spoke to the teams about the economic and social injustices of their employment, they listened. When he told them they would have to challenge the authority of the club owners, the black and Hispanic players were ready.

Miller's objections to the reserve clause were twofold. On economic grounds, the clause artificially lowered players' salaries. Without competitive bidding to determine a player's value, his earnings were set by fiat of the club. The player's only recourse would be to sit out, a generally unfeasible option.

To some extent, the introduction of salary arbitration in 1973 alleviated the economic problem. With that step, an impartial party could consider the merits of each side's salary proposal and determine which one would prevail in the player's next contract. But the reserve clause remained offensive because of its inherent unfairness. Miller stressed that aside from the economic problems, the reserve clause precluded an essential American freedom: the right of a worker and an employer to agree to a hiring.

Curt Flood's challenge to the reserve clause coincided with Miller's efforts for black and Hispanic players. The Flood case clarified the injustice of clubs controlling players. In his letter to Commissioner Bowie Kuhn, Flood made clear that his reasons for rejecting his trade from the Cardinals to the Phillies concerned justice more than money:[11]

Beyond the Plantation Game

Dear Mr. Kuhn:

After 12 years in the major leagues, I do not feel that I am a piece of property to be bought and sold irrespective of my wishes. I believe that any system that produces that result violates my basic rights as a citizen and is inconsistent with the laws of the United States and of several states.

It is my desire to play baseball in 1970 and I am capable of playing. I have received a contract from the Philadelphia club, but I believe I have the right to reconsider offers from other clubs before making any decisions. I, therefore, request that you make known to all the major league clubs my feelings in this matter, and advise them of my availability for the 1970 season.

Curt Flood

In a telling reply, Kuhn began with a "Dear Curt" salutation that the commissioner later acknowledged in his memoir was taken by the Players Association to reflect a "plantation mentality." On the merits of Flood's case, Kuhn wrote, "I certainly agree with you that you, as a human being, are not a piece of property to be bought and sold. That is fundamental in our society and I think obvious. However, I cannot see its applicability to the situation at hand."[12]

Kuhn continued that Flood's contract included the necessary legal authority for the Cardinals to trade him as they saw fit. In his memoir, Kuhn recognized that some modification of the reserve clause was inevitable, but he did not believe that the court was the proper instrument for the adjustment.

The federal courts sustained the reserve clause while noting that it was an aberration to hold baseball exempt from antitrust law. The court had previously looked to Congress to make any needed correction, and in the absence of a legislative remedy, the courts refused to intervene.

While the legal machinations of the Flood case were tangled, the social significance is clear. Among the specifics of Flood's complaint, he alleged that the reserve clause imposed

39

a condition of involuntary servitude in violation of the Thirteenth Amendment's ban on slavery.

The federal district court rejected the slavery argument because there was no "showing of compulsory service." Strictly speaking, this was true—no one was forcing Flood to play baseball. But within the profession of baseball, a strangling restriction of freedom of movement prevailed.

Justice Thurgood Marshall, the Supreme Court's only black justice, picked this point up in his dissent when he wrote, "To non-athletes it might appear that petitioner was virtually enslaved by the owners of major league baseball clubs who bartered among themselves for his services."[13]

Although the legal arguments were unsuccessful, they clarified the nature of progress for blacks in baseball. Barred until 1947, black players had infused the game with some of its greatest talent during the 1950s and 1960s. They contributed to the game's popularity and to the money that consequently poured into the owners' treasuries.

Black players could see that they had been admitted to an industry that relied on a caste system, and the achievement of Jackie Robinson and his fellows was to integrate the lower class. Baseball was not truly a capitalist industry with a natural gap in compensation between employers and employees. Instead, the business was much like a plantation economy with great social, as well as economic, distinctions between the owners and the players.

In the 1970s, the players would challenge the nature of their relationship with the owners. Miller remembers that most of the players came from families that had no union background and that many of the white players had been raised to be deferential to coaches and others in authority. After many years of struggle against oppression, black players were more attuned to the union's call.

The legacy of slavery, segregation, and bigotry gave black players a special perspective when they were sold to a team in another town and were forced to relocate their families. The insane refusal to admit blacks to the game produced skepticism about the owners' judgment while baseball slowly integrated from 1947 to 1959. The hatred that black players encountered even until the 1970s confirmed that no one had done these men a favor by allowing them to play professional baseball—they were on the field because they put fans in the seats and money in the owners' pockets. This special perspective provided a kind of kindling when Miller lit the spark of the players' revolt.

With some exceptions, the game of baseball is free from the shackles of racism, and the myth that teams will put the best players on the field in pursuit of victory is finally reality. But the business of baseball continues to show that racism lives as a virus in today's society: it is often dormant, but under the right conditions, it can erupt in a virulent form.

Few people had noticed baseball's obstacles that kept blacks from management positions in major league franchises. The subject did not receive a great deal of attention until 1987, when Al Campanis, the general manager of the Dodgers, expounded at length on network television about why few blacks made it to the front offices of baseball.

His remarks that blacks lacked the "necessities"—that they might not be able to serve as executives any more than they could swim— exposed an Archie Bunker mentality in the inner circle of one of baseball's most glamorous franchises. Within a day, Campanis was an object of derision and was unemployed. His remarks were so inflammatory that baseball's public relations crisis overwhelmed the original question: Why are so few blacks hired as managers and executives?

To answer that blacks are rarely hired because baseball is a racist institution is a weak response. Racism in baseball is not the rigorously enforced conscious conspiracy that prevailed before 1947; rather, it is that old subtle bias that blinds club executives to the availability of talented men and women.

In the aftermath of the Campanis fiasco, a conscious strategy to improve minority representation led to some highly publicized hirings, including Bill White—president of the National League; Tommy Hawkins—vice president of communications for the Dodgers; Bob Watson—assistant general manager of Houston; and Elaine Weddington—assistant general manager of the Red Sox. The limitation of a policy that sets out to hire people of a specific race, sex, or ethnicity is the danger that the employer acts out of a sense of obligation rather than self-interest.

If blacks, Hispanics, and women receive opportunities in executive positions in baseball because the owners think it is good public relations or even the right thing to do, then a critical lesson of baseball's history of racism will have been lost. Bigotry weakens its perpetrator as well as its object, and the same can be said for the milder form of racism that is indifference.

Baseball is currently concerned with the impression that it is losing the allegiance of black fans. With teams desperate for new sources of revenue, clubs take few specific efforts to market the game to black fans. Don Newcombe estimates that the Dodgers sell fewer season tickets to blacks than do the Lakers of the National Basketball Association. The data are unavailable to confirm or refute Newcombe's impression, but because the former Cy Young winner and MVP believes it to be true, baseball may have a significant problem: an estrangement between those who market baseball and some of the players who are best able to draw fans to the game.

Peter Bavasi explains the absence of blacks in executive positions in baseball in a larger economic context.[14] Bavasi grew up in baseball, running minor league teams for the Dodgers while his father, Buzzie, served as the team's general manager, and later Peter ran several major league clubs himself.

As the younger Bavasi sees it, the failure to hire blacks as managers and coaches is inexcusable. The requisite skills are a knowledge of the game and an ability to communicate that to players. He points out that any number of black ex-players have those skills in abundance. One wrinkle in hiring some better-known retired players is that players' salaries are now so high that going to the minor leagues as a coach for a few years of apprenticeship appeals to fewer players than it once did.

The front office jobs may be another matter. They have become, in Bavasi's view, fundamentally different than what they used to be. No longer is the general manager a former player who worked for a few years as a field manager before the burden of travel became too much. The financial pressures on the clubs now require that club executives have strong business skills, and Bavasi doubts that many former players of any ethnic or racial background fit that bill.

He notes that few former players are in key front office positions these days, and he also points to the number of general managers being fired as a sign of the new importance of the position and its relationship with the clubs' financial picture. If baseball has to improve its business operations, then it needs to recruit beyond an old buddy system of ex-players.

Finding qualified black business executives gives baseball a problem and an opportunity. The problem is that it must compete with every other company in America for that talent, but the opportunity is that the game is no longer so tied to those few men who played.

John Young may prove to be one test of baseball's sincerity in hiring black executives.[15] Young is a forty-three-year-old scout for the Florida Marlins, recently moving to the expansion team after serving in the same post with the Texas Rangers. Young is pursuing a studiously prepared route to the front office. After examining the careers of successful general managers like Pat Gillick and Bill Lajoie, Young concludes that the path to executive positions is through a slow and thorough preparation in a variety of jobs. In that vein, Young notes that nineteen of the twenty-six current general managers had experience as scouts, Young's current job.

One of the obstacles to that path for aspiring blacks is a double standard that Young believes still affects baseball. The marginal white player may have a chance to work his way up through an organization, but, when hiring blacks, clubs tend to think of superstars who provide immediate visibility.

The retired great player who is black may not have had the opportunity to learn the craft of being a baseball executive. Young insists that being a good general manager does not depend so much on an ability to assess baseball talent but on the good judgment to hire the right people and to know the strengths of different minor leagues so that the reports that are received about a prospect can be sensibly assessed.

One of Peter Bavasi's points is pertinent here. A player like Young, who appeared only briefly in the major leagues, might be interested in staying in the game by working long hours on the road to get to know people throughout organized baseball. But any player who starred for a number of years and who made a substantial salary in the game is not so likely to find that painstaking path appealing.

Young has another interest that may be crucial to the future of baseball. He organized a program called Reviving Baseball in Inner-cities (RBI) to develop an interest in baseball among black youngsters. Unlike Little League, RBI is targeted to minority youngsters who might otherwise not be able to play ball under adult supervision. The goal of RBI is not so much to attract future players as it is to promote values of sportsmanship among children and adolescents who may never make a major league roster but who might become season-ticket holders.

The great black prospect needs little encouragement from Young or RBI, because plenty of teams will find that talent and try to develop it. Similarly, in the tragic communities of the inner cities, some children suffer from problems that are beyond the power of baseball to change. But Young is convinced that there are a tremendous number of young men and women who are on the fence and who might decide to stay with school and pursue serious careers if they receive the kind of attention that RBI can offer.

The program began in Southern California, and it has been copied in several cities across the country. The commissioner of baseball has taken an interest in it, and its future appears to be promising. This special attention is essential because blanket approaches to attracting young players and fans to baseball have limited utility in the black community.

Whatever success RBI enjoys, the virus of racism will again erupt in baseball unless a fundamental change in perspective occurs in those who run the game. The moral arguments that inevitably follow something like the Campanis flap are helpful but insufficient. If the owners could appreciate that their own limitations in this area have cost them money, pennants, and skilled employees, they could see that even in its less malignant forms racism is bad business.

Since the 1960s, America's racial climate has increasingly been understood from different perspectives. Polls have demonstrated how sharply black and white Americans differ on issues like affirmative action, racial quotas, police behavior, and other controversies. In general, white America is proud of and somewhat content with the racial progress to date while black Americans remain troubled by the fears and hostility that they see permeating the culture.

To promote racial justice, businesses cannot be content with numbers that purport to demonstrate progress. More blacks than ever have executive positions in baseball, but perhaps more important, former players like Henry Aaron seem to get more frustrated and angry each year. When Aaron says, as he did on "Nightline" in 1991, that nothing has changed since 1947, he is factually incorrect. But his saying and believing such a thing is compelling evidence that baseball still has a very serious racial problem.

In the future, the challenge of racial justice may become more complex for baseball and other businesses and institutions. Stephen Carter, Shelby Steele, and Thomas Sowell are a few of the more notable black men who are challenging the value of affirmative action programs to promote economic and social progress. The one black man now on the Supreme Court, Clarence Thomas, holds distinctly different views on some issues than did the only other black man, Thurgood Marshall, ever to sit on that bench. Arguments about quotas and diversity are likely to be soon exposed as ultimately sterile.

Fay Vincent and Bill White have encouraged clubs to hire minority talent, but the record in 1991 is dismal. Half the managerial positions in baseball were vacant, and black representation remained at one. Two new franchises were added to the National League, but minority hirings for their front offices were low level and scarce. Even more troubling is the impression that blacks were not seriously considered for many of these positions.

Perhaps a meritocracy is operating with the most talented people, who happen to be white men, prevailing. If so, that is a defensible if unsettling outcome. But if managers start being fired left and right and the expansion teams stumble for years, fair-minded people will have reason to ask if baseball is a meritocracy or a torpid institution.

Racial justice has proven to be good business. To the extent that the ideal has been realized, the business of baseball has profited immensely. If black Americans—as players, fans, and executives—abandon baseball for other sports, the loss to the game could be devastating. Some great black stars will remain, so we will never again be so blind as people were before 1947. But the postwar game that now tugs at our emotions may eventually stand out as a uniquely rich period in the history of the sport, because that was the time that baseball was the place to go for the great black athlete.

NOTES

1. See, for example, Jules Tygiel, *Baseball's Great Experiment* (New York: Oxford University Press, 1985).

2. Robert Peterson, *Only the Ball Was White* (New York: McGraw-Hill, 1970), pp. 173–74.
3. Bill Veeck, *Veeck as in Wreck* (New York: Fireside, 1989), p. 171.
4. This record of major league integration is taken from Merl Kleinknecht, "Integration of Baseball After World War II," *Baseball Research Journal*, Society of American Baseball Research, 1983, pp. 100–106.
5. Attendance figures from the *Sporting News*.
6. Donald J. Bogue, *The Population of the United States: Historical Trends and Future Projections* (New York: Free Press, 1985), pp. 710–11.
7. Don Newcombe, interview, Dodger Stadium, August 21, 1990.
8. Al Rosen, interview by telephone, June 14, 1991.
9. Donald Fehr, interview, Fehr's office, June 24, 1991.
10. Marvin Miller, interview, Miller's home, March 21, 1991.
11. Bowie Kuhn, *Hardball: The Education of a Baseball Commissioner* (New York: Times Books, 1987), p. 83.
12. Ibid.
13. *Flood* v. *Kuhn*, 407 U.S. 258, 1972, p. 290.
14. Peter Bavasi, interview, Bavasi's office, June 26, 1991.
15. John Young, interview, July 3, 1991.

3

Portable
Franchises

At midcentury, the gap between rich and poor franchises was so wide that a few of the marginal clubs bolted from their historic homes to more promising markets. Forty years after those first moves, the issue of economic imbalance among the major league franchises is more contentious than ever because the owners have not yet reconciled their common needs with their personal desires.

Clubs have moved for a variety of reasons. In the first instances, clubs felt squeezed by another team that shared their town. Other teams have headed for untapped territory in the belief that the simple act of showing up would make them richer. Stadium deals and television contracts have lured other clubs, and some terrific baseball towns have been abused in the bargain.

Moving a franchise to improve its earnings has almost always been a mistake born of the false conclusion that the abandoned community will no longer support baseball. When the real problems have been mismanagement, relocation has offered little or no respite, and the financial imbalances among the major league clubs continue as before.

Through fifty years, from 1903 to 1953, the sixteen major league teams had remained in ten cities in the East and the

Midwest. Several franchises had bordered on bankruptcy during that time, but the temptation to move to more lucrative markets was rarely entertained.

The placement of major league teams that stabilized in 1903 made considerable sense for the urban populations of the day. The census of 1900 shows the rank of the ten cities that would be homes to major league baseball over the next half-century.

1900 City Populations vs. Major League Team Locations

CITY	POPULATION IN 1900[1]	NUMBER OF MAJOR LEAGUE TEAMS
New York	3,437,202	3
Chicago	1,698,575	2
Philadelphia	1,293,697	2
St. Louis	575,238	2
Boston	560,892	2
Baltimore	508,957	0
Cleveland	381,768	1
Buffalo	352,387	0
San Francisco	342,782	0
Cincinnati	325,902	1
Pittsburgh	321,616	1
New Orleans	287,104	0
Detroit	285,704	1
Milwaukee	285,315	0
Washington, D.C.	278,718	1

Of the six cities with populations greater than half a million, five were given teams in both the American and the National League, except for Baltimore, which is 45 miles from Washington, D.C., and 143 miles from Philadelphia. San Francisco and New Orleans were also left out, but they were too remote for the transportation of that day. Buffalo and Milwaukee could have made strong pitches for inclusion, but they had been bypassed when the Western League made its transformation into the American League by shifting franchises to eastern markets.

In a century of migration, these markets were inevitably affected. Two world wars and the Great Depression were the most dramatic factors in driving people from their homes in flight from desperation or in search of new opportunity. Jobs in factories in the North attracted migrants from the South. The promise of a good life in California drew the poor that John Steinbeck championed in *The Grapes of Wrath*. Many veterans of World War II remembered the mild winters that they had enjoyed in the West before they shipped out to the Pacific. They returned in droves to the burgeoning communities of the West Coast.

The census of 1950 showed the cracks in baseball's old order:

1950 City Populations vs. Major League Team Locations

CITY	POPULATION IN 1950	NUMBER OF MAJOR LEAGUE TEAMS
New York	7,891,957	3
Chicago	3,620,962	2
Philadelphia	2,071,605	2
Los Angeles	1,970,358	0
Detroit	1,849,568	1
Baltimore	949,708	0
Cleveland	914,808	1
St. Louis	856,796	2
Washington, D.C.	802,178	1
Boston	801,444	2
San Francisco	775,357	0
Pittsburgh	676,808	1
Milwaukee	637,392	0
Houston	596,163	0
Buffalo	580,132	0
New Orleans	570,445	0
Minneapolis	521,718	0
Cincinnati	503,998	1

Portable Franchises

On the face of it, the alignment at midcentury was distorted. How profitably could two teams operate in Boston and St. Louis? In an age of air travel, how could Los Angeles continue to be ignored when it had a market four times the size of Cincinnati? Los Angeles improved San Francisco's prospects for a team because clubs going to California would find it economical to make a second stop in the West.

As airline travel brought America's cities closer to one another, the automobile sent the old eastern cities into decline by facilitating flight to the suburbs. The GI Bill, urban renewal, the highway program, and other government policies enticed families from the inner cities and made suburban living irresistible. The economic pressure became unbearable for the old distribution of clubs.

The league alignments of 1903 collapsed suddenly in the 1950s, and over the next twenty years baseball adjusted to ten significant franchise moves. The public reaction to those moves is another indication of the business changes in baseball. What was first a cause for bitter muttering at the local pub has become a provocation for legal and political action that could block future attempts to move franchises.

The first few moves broke the hearts of a small band of loyal fans whose distress was largely ignored. The demise of the Boston Braves, the St. Louis Browns, and the Philadelphia Athletics drew small wakes, but the move west of the Dodgers traumatized the entire borough of Brooklyn and produced a virtual branch of literature to release the agony of Flatbush. Yet a generation of New Yorkers have largely missed the most important lessons about Brooklyn's loss.

As city governments became more directly involved in attracting and holding ball clubs, the hurt feelings of fans became the outrage of citizens and taxpayers. When the unremarkable Seattle Pilots jumped to Milwaukee after just one season, the city neither pined nor cursed. It threatened to sue, and it received a replacement expansion club for its efforts.

51

Sports franchises have accepted public largesse, especially in the form of publicly financed stadiums and arenas, and this gives the community a very tangible interest in the decision of a club owner to keep his team in its traditional home or to look for a more lucrative market. To protect community interests, legislation has been proposed in Congress to restrict franchise moves.[2] These bills have raised some fundamental and intriguing questions about the relationship between teams and communities and the rights and responsibilities of fans and their teams.

From 1953 to 1972, clubs tumbled after one another reacting to the changing demographics of postwar America. The St. Louis Browns' financial plight caused owner Bill Veeck to try to move the club to Milwaukee, where he had owned the Brewers of the American Association in the early 1940s.[3] The other owners refused to permit the move, but they did allow Lou Perini to take the Braves from Boston to Milwaukee just a month before the 1953 season despite the disruption of schedules.

When August Busch, with the deep pockets of the Anheuser-Busch brewery, purchased the Cardinals in 1954, Veeck was doomed in St. Louis. He was forced to sell the club to interests who moved it to Baltimore. The byzantine moves of the owners accomplished three objectives. First, the Boston and St. Louis markets that were seen to be saturated were pruned. Second, major league baseball expanded to new territory that had been prepared for generations by successful minor league operations. Finally, and perhaps most important, Bill Veeck was out of baseball. The fraternity had been purged of its least conforming member.

The entangled affairs of the owners were evident again when Connie Mack's family sold the Athletics to Arnold Johnson. Johnson was a business associate of Dan Topping's and Del Webb's, the owners of the Yankees. Johnson bought the rights to the Kansas City territory from the Yankees, and he moved the Athletics to the Midwest to play in a stadium that had just been renovated by Webb's construction company. The commercial circle was complete when Johnson later was awarded concession contracts at Yankee Stadium.

The New York Giants (1958) moved because Horace Stoneham could not make money in New York with Willie Mays in his prime and Orlando Cepeda, Willie McCovey, and Juan Marichal ready to join the team. The prosperous Brooklyn Dodgers (1958) headed west to build the stadium of Walter O'Malley's dreams.

The Washington Senators (1961) concluded that the nation's capital was hopeless, and they fled to Minnesota. Two clubs became peripatetic, moving for a second time in a generation: The Milwaukee Braves (1966) jumped to Atlanta, and the Kansas City Athletics (1968) moved to Oakland. After a single season, the Seattle Pilots (1970) became the Milwaukee Brewers, but not before Jim Bouton revolutionized baseball literature. The Washington Senators II (1972) gave up on the District and headed for Dallas–Ft. Worth.

The franchise moves of the 1950s delivered instant prosperity. As the clubs required more and more money to operate, struggling owners looked to relocation as a means to stay in the game, and, for a time, franchise moves provided a dramatic shot in the arm to the itinerant club:

Team Attendance: Old vs. New Markets, 1952–58

TEAM	ATTENDANCE: LAST YEAR IN OLD MARKET		ATTENDANCE: FIRST YEAR IN NEW MARKET	
Braves	Boston	1952—281,278	Milwaukee	1953—1,826,397
Orioles	St. Louis	1953—297,238	Baltimore	1954—1,060,910
Athletics	Phila.	1954—304,666	K.C.	1955—1,393,054
Dodgers	Bklyn.	1957—1,028,528	L.A.	1958—1,845,556
Giants	New York	1957—653,923	S.F.	1958—1,272,625
Twins	Wash.	1960—743,404	Minn.	1961—1,256,723

THE DIAMOND REVOLUTION

Each of these clubs, except the Dodgers, was purported to be losing money, if the machinations of baseball accounting can be trusted. Each franchise found virgin territory where enthusiasm for major league baseball overwhelmed whatever management deficiencies had led to problems in the old markets.

By the mid-1960s, the novelty of major league baseball had run its course in Milwaukee and Kansas City, and fans in those cities needed to be drawn to the park through competitive clubs and effective marketing. The Braves still had players from their pennant-winning teams, and, while younger talent was needed, Henry Aaron was only midway through his career home run record. Despite never having suffered a losing season in Milwaukee, the Braves moved to Atlanta for the 1966 season. Not since Horace Stoneham took Willie Mays to San Francisco has a move made less economic sense.

The initial results of the Braves' second move were encouraging. Their attendance jumped by about one million over the last year in Milwaukee, but that improvement was very short-lived. By the measure of attendance, the Braves' move to Atlanta was a great mistake:

Braves Attendance Before and After 1966 Move

IN MILWAUKEE		IN ATLANTA			
YEAR	ATTENDANCE	YEAR	ATTENDANCE	YEAR	ATTENDANCE
1953	1,826,397	1966	1,539,801	1979	769,465
1954	2,131,388	1967	1,389,222	1980	1,048,411
1955	2,005,836	1968	1,126,540	1981	535,418
1956	2,046,331	1969	1,458,320	1982	1,801,985
1957	2,215,404	1970	1,078,848	1983	2,119,935
1958	1,971,101	1971	1,006,320	1984	1,724,892
1959	1,749,112	1972	752,973	1985	1,350,137
1960	1,497,799	1973	800,655	1986	1,387,181
1961	1,101,441	1974	981,085	1987	1,217,402
1962	766,921	1975	534,672	1988	848,089
1963	773,018	1976	818,179	1989	984,930
1964	910,911	1977	872,464	1990	980,129
1965	555,584	1978	904,494	1991	2,140,217

Portable Franchises

The jump to Atlanta had some short-term benefits, as they were the South's first team. But the Braves have topped two million in attendance only twice in Atlanta, after doing so four times during their thirteen-year visit to Milwaukee. Even the championship team of 1991 fell short of the attendance mark of the 1957 Milwaukee Braves.

A good team in the early 1980s boosted the Braves' attendance over the two million mark in 1983 and kept the gate at more than a million until 1988. The doormat team of the National League West until 1991, the Braves have been barely able to draw more fans in the late 1980s than saw the team in their final years in Milwaukee.

Comparing the totals, the Braves drew 19,551,243 fans during their thirteen-year stay in Milwaukee, for an average annual attendance of 1,503,942. The first thirteen years in Atlanta drew 13,263,573, for a yearly average of 1,020,275. This disparity exists even though Atlanta is about 25% larger than Milwaukee.

Attendance, of course, is not the sole indicator of a team's success. It is no longer even the primary source of a club's revenue. In moving from Milwaukee to Atlanta, the Braves left a small market hemmed between Chicago and Minneapolis–St. Paul for a regional market in which they represented the entire South. The broadcasting and licensing advantages are apparent, but they may remain illusory if the team is unappealing, and that is where attendance becomes important beyond its own revenues.

The Braves have had a desultory appearance when they have played before a virtually empty house. Sponsors and logos are easier to sell when the team is exciting, and a packed house is one of the best signs of an exciting ball club. Playing in an empty cavern, whether in Atlanta or Cleveland, is not going to cause fans to rush to the store and buy a team cap.

After the Braves moved to the South, the big leagues were represented in every quadrant of the country but the Northwest. The significance is that any further franchise movement would face some kind of competition from an existing team. The excitement of being a region's first major league club would no longer be a factor in a team's popularity, and the attendance figures for the remaining moves of major league franchises reflect that lack of innocent enthusiasm.

Team Attendance: Old vs. New Markets, 1967–72

TEAM	LAST YEAR IN OLD MARKET		FIRST YEAR IN NEW MARKET	
Athletics	K.C.	1967—726,639	Oakland	1968—837,466
Brewers	Seattle	1969—677,944	Milwaukee	1970—933,690
Rangers	Wash.	1971—655,156	Texas	1972—662,974

The Athletics are an instructive case. When they moved from Philadelphia to Kansas City in 1955, they picked up more than one million new fans in their first season in the Midwest. They struggled on the field, but by the mid-1960s they were in the hands of a new owner, Charlie Finley, who was nothing if not innovative in marketing. Exotic uniform colors, a pop-up rabbit to resupply baseballs, and a grazing goat were a few of the novelties that Finley brought to the game. Unfortunately, the ball club was poor. They continued to rest near the bottom of the American League and remained a poor draw.

When Finley moved the Athletics to Oakland thirteen years after they had left Philadelphia, they arrived in an area that had been host to the Giants for a decade. The gain in attendance for the Athletics from their second move was less than 100,000 new fans.

Finley's marketing was certainly radical, but it was not particularly good. Even when he compiled one of the great teams in the history of the game, the A's drew poorly in Oakland for a club that was winning three consecutive world championships. The promise of that club was evident in 1969 when it finished second in the first year of divisional play, yet attendance dropped from 837,466 in 1968 to 778,232 the following year. The record after that is amazing:

Portable Franchises

Oakland A's Finishes and Attendance, 1970–75

YEAR	FINISH	RECORD	GAMES AHEAD OR BACK	ATTENDANCE
1970	2nd	89–73	−9 GB	778,355
1971	1st	101–60	+16	914,993
1972	1st*	93–62	+5.5	921,323
1973	1st*	94–68	+6	1,000,763
1974	1st*	90–72	+5	845,693
1975	1st	98–64	+7	1,075,518

* World Championships

The A's have been the only club since the Yankees dynasty to win three world championships in succession, but they drew miserably during those tremendous seasons. In Reggie Jackson, Jim "Catfish" Hunter, Vida Blue, Sal Bando, Joe Rudi, Gene Tenace, Rollie Fingers, and so many others, they had one of the most colorful groups since the Gashouse Gang. But they still could not draw flies.

When the A's rebounded in the late 1980s, attendance in the range of 2.5 million became routine. Finley could judge talent, and he was quite adept at challenging the conventions of the game; but he failed to attract the fans of Oakland to the brilliant team that he assembled.

The instant fix that the moves of the 1950s generated contributed to a nefarious excuse that is still occasionally invoked: that a particular community is a "bad baseball town." The critical implication is that the front office, the manager, and the players are all above reproach, but something is seriously wrong with the fans who fail to support the club adequately.

Horace Stoneham made the point about New York when asked at the time of the Giants' move if he felt bad for the team's young fans. Stoneham replied that he did but that he had not seen much of their fathers lately.

Washington, D.C., Cleveland, Pittsburgh, and Seattle are

just some of the communities that have worn this tag recently. But that "bad baseball town" theory is a poor excuse that tries to cover failures of management. The club may have been poorly marketed, played in a stadium that is decrepit or in a dangerous part of town, or lost popular players via trades or free agency. The notion that fans in a particular city are impervious to the charms of baseball is belied by two facts.

First, no city has lost a team without retaining another club or securing a new one through expansion. Five of the first ten expansion teams since 1961 have been located in cities that have been abandoned by another major league club. If the problem with the departed club was really the community, why risk a new franchise in such an unpromising site? Some replacement teams arrive so fast that there is scarcely time for a decent wake.

Cities Losing a Franchise and Acquiring Another

CITY	ABANDONED BY	REPLACED WITH
New York	Dodgers & Giants 1958	Mets 1962
Washington, D.C.	Senators 1961	Senators II 1961
Washington, D.C.	Senators II 1972	——
Milwaukee	Braves 1966	Brewers 1970
Kansas City	Athletics 1968	Royals 1969
Seattle	Pilots 1970	Mariners 1977

The attendance for some of those expansion teams is the second fact that undermines the "bad town" explanation of a struggling baseball club. The record (see table, page 59) demonstrates clearly that expansion franchises that replaced a departed team generally draw much better than the old club does in what it thought would be greener pastures.

The expansion record is especially damning with regard to the Giants, who should never have left New York; the Braves, who should have stayed in Milwaukee; and the Athletics, who should have remained in Kansas City. Sweeter stadium and

Portable Franchises
Number of Years with Greater Attendance

YEARS	TRANSFERRED CLUB IN ITS NEW MARKET		EXPANSION CLUB IN ABANDONED MARKET	
1962–91	Giants	5	Mets	24
1969–91	A's	6	Royals	16
1969–91	Braves	8	Brewers	14
1961–71	Twins	11	Senators II	0
1977–91	Brewers	12	Mariners	2

broadcast deals might have provided the financial impulse for these moves, but the Mets, the Brewers, and the Royals have trounced their predecessors in attendance races, salvaging the cities' reputations as communities that will support baseball.

Washington, D.C., failed to attract one of the new National League expansion clubs, and the nation's capital seems burdened by the history of two franchises that left town. But the biggest obstacle to baseball in Washington may be the impression that much of the city is a war zone of competing drug gangs. Locating a stadium in one of the Virginia suburbs would probably be a more prudent step if baseball ever returns to the capital, but a change in some prevailing attitudes may also be necessary.

Peter Bavasi recounts that during his tenure with the San Diego Padres, the club was once on the verge of moving to Washington, D.C.[4] Bavasi went through the abandoned offices of the Texas Rangers at RFK Stadium to get a list of season-ticket holders. After an unsuccessful search, he called the Rangers to find where the list was filed.

He was told not to bother, because the more important list in Washington was the roster of government officials who expected complimentary seats. So ended the brief history of the Washington Padres.

At this writing, the major league owners are wrestling with the issue of whether to admit to their ranks Japan's Nintendo

Corporation, which is trying to buy the Seattle Mariners. Commissioner Fay Vincent responded to the first reports of the offer with deep skepticism that the owners would approve the transfer. Some critics of Vincent and the owners have charged that racism is the reason for rebuffing Nintendo, and, based on baseball's history, that charge cannot be dismissed out of hand.

Factors other than xenophobia may explain the reluctance to welcome Japanese money. One is that current owners (Bill Veeck being a clear exception) are generally supported when they choose to sell or move their franchise, and Jeff Smulyan would make significantly more money selling the Mariners to a Tampa-St. Petersburg contingent than to one based in Seattle. If Smulyan has been a loyal frat brother, the owners' club would likely rally to him.

More significant for baseball's future, the owners may simply lack the vision to include foreign ownership at this time. The major league owners have been exceedingly reluctant to expand their own ranks, to share power with the players, and they have used all of their advantages to subordinate any competition from minor league clubs. Suddenly to embrace the expansion beyond the shores of the English-speaking parts of North America may require more mettle than the owners possess. The future prosperity of baseball may well depend on bridging to an international game, but, as Al Campanis might say, the current crop of owners may lack the necessities to pursue that course.

In considering the case of the Mariners and all other possible franchise shifts, one move continues to have a momentous hold on the business of baseball. Generations have passed since the Dodgers left Brooklyn, but the legend of the move only grows.[5] Fans who were not born when the demolition crew razed Ebbets Field keen about their loss. Passed on like an epic poem in the oral tradition of Flatbush is the tragic saga of postwar baseball:

Portable Franchises

After decades of struggle in the shadows of the lordly Yankees and Giants, the Dodgers emerged with one of the great teams in the game's history during the 1950s. The Boys of Summer were not only a terrific ball club, but they were an important moral force for giving blacks an opportunity to play.

Ebbets Field was the perfect setting for these heroes. The park was gracious and intimate, with a charming assortment of eccentricities—the Abe Stark sign, the hit-error designation in the Schaefer beer ad, the beveled base of the right-field wall, the notch in dead center.

The park was invariably jammed to capacity, but you could still walk up and get a great seat whenever the mood struck. After Robinson broke in, blacks and whites sat together in joyful brotherhood bound by their common love of the Dodgers.

The excruciating pennant races, playoffs, and World Series frustrations of the postwar era were finally swept aside by the team's gutty championship in 1955. Johnny Podres's 2–0 shutout in the seventh game in Yankee Stadium put the lie to the whispers and self-doubts that the Dodgers choked in big games.

With the monkey finally off their backs, a front office betrayal of unimagined proportions began to unfold. Back in 1950, Walter Francis O'Malley had forced Branch Rickey out of the Dodgers organization. By the mid-1950s, the corpulent, jowly, gravel-voiced, cigar-smoking owner was dropping hints that Ebbets Field would not be the Dodgers' home beyond the immediate future.

O'Malley tried to con New York officials into building a new stadium for the Dodgers and giving it to the club. Reasonable counteroffers were made, but O'Malley was not interested. Conceivably, the demand for a new stadium was simply a ruse to cover the negotiations with Los Angeles, where O'Malley had intended to move all along. He was eager to leave New York because he anticipated the hard times that would befall the city, leading up to the fiscal crisis of the 1970s.

The appeal of Los Angeles shows O'Malley's evil genius.

THE DIAMOND REVOLUTION

The attendance of the Pacific Coast League teams in the town had been dropping sharply during the 1950s, but O'Malley somehow knew that his team would draw three million fans even during an average season.

After turning his New York ways on the bumpkins in Los Angeles, O'Malley was handed the exclusive property at Chavez Ravine. When the gas lines formed across the country during the 1970s, another feature of the Chavez Ravine deal received wider attention—O'Malley got the mineral rights from the city. His stadium was sitting atop a Permian Basin of oil in the middle of Los Angeles.

Having secured his own aims, O'Malley then contrived an even crueler fate for New York. To secure league approval for his move, he needed another team to go to the Coast to make the travel costs less burdensome. Who better to take along than the Giants? The rivalry would continue in California, further enhancing O'Malley's profits and costing New York the Say Hey Kid.

With the Los Angeles offer in hand, O'Malley waited for the right moment to twist the knife into Brooklyn. He found it during the 1957 World Series, when Red Patterson, the team's press liaison, read an innocuous announcement about "drafting the Los Angeles territory" that couched the betrayal in obscurity.

O'Malley flew to Los Angeles with his bewildered players to rake in his millions. Brooklyn fans were left with poignant memories and shattered dreams.

One has to be impressed with the tale. It is elegant in form, filled with sympathetic victims and a mendacious villain, and it delivers a powerful moral that if club owners are not appeased by their communities, they will abandon them without a second thought. The tale is also patently false.

The story is so appealing that one could forgive its inaccuracies if a healthy lesson were derived by the listeners, but that has not been the case. Public officials all over the country have rushed to placate club owners under the rhetoric of economic development and community pride. In fact, the principal economic development has been the fattening of the teams' treasuries in an unseemly exercise that precludes any semblance of community pride.

To clarify the record, begin with the assumption that O'Malley was as greedy as his fiercest critics charge. Why would he abruptly move the most prosperous franchise in baseball 1,500 miles beyond the westernmost outpost of the major leagues? Why move to a city that had beaches, mountains, the desert, and other free entertainment? Why leave a market that had been extremely lucrative, with established rivalries and the greatest population base in the country?

That O'Malley's appearance and manner were central casting's caricature of a corporate villain is beyond dispute. That he was fond of the dollar is also not questioned. But the obsession with the personality and character of Walter O'Malley has distracted people from the facts of the Dodgers' move and from the pertinent lessons that remain important for us.

The truth is that, consistent with his fondness for the dollar, O'Malley was looking to build his own stadium whose design, use, ticket prices, and maintenance he could control. He stated clearly that he did not want to be a tenant in a political ball park.

He found a spot for his new stadium in the borough of Brooklyn, at the intersection of Atlantic and Flatbush avenues. The neighborhood includes the junction of two subway lines and a terminal for the Long Island Rail Road. It also could have accommodated far more cars than the seven hundred that could park by Ebbets Field. The site would have been an ideal location for a modern urban ball park in New York, and the land would have been purchased by the Dodgers.

To acquire the site, O'Malley needed the city of New York, and specifically Robert Moses, to assemble the various plots of land into a single parcel that he could afford. Such action would have been consistent with urban renewal projects of the day.

Moses, the architect of New York's infrastructure in the twentieth century, wanted to build what became Shea Stadium, a public facility in the borough of Queens. O'Malley had no interest in having Moses for his landlord. The two powerful figures were unable to reach an accommodation, and O'Malley's hopes for a private stadium in Brooklyn were scuttled.

The probing, bargaining, ultimatums, and other negotiating ploys unfolded over months and years, but O'Malley's goal to build a new stadium in Brooklyn with his own money was prevented from the start by the political decisions of New York City officials. In the end, he could have stayed in Ebbets Field or moved to Queens, but neither choice was acceptable to him.

On the West Coast, Los Angeles officials were hardly conned by O'Malley. They had been trying for years to get rid of the city-owned property at Chavez Ravine. Before it was transformed into one of the great sites in baseball, the land consisted of hills and gullies, and it was home to a small Hispanic community. The land was taken by the city for a federal housing project that never materialized. It was returned to the city, rather than to the residents, with the instructions from the federal government that the site be put to a public purpose. To that end, the city tried without success to entice developers with ideas from a cemetery to an opera house.

O'Malley first saw Chavez Ravine during a layover on the Dodgers' trip to Japan after the 1956 World Series. Some accounts contend that O'Malley decided then and there to move the club to Los Angeles. Even if that is true, the city's first formal offer to the Dodgers, made during spring training of 1957, was quashed by the Los Angeles city attorney in May of that year, when he determined that the terms of the deal were illegal. Even if O'Malley thought in October 1956 that he was moving, serious discussions between Los Angeles and the Dodgers did not begin until the summer of 1957.

After months of discussions, an agreement was reached that would transfer the city's property at Chavez Ravine for the Dodgers' minor league ball park, Wrigley Field. The contract then barely cleared procedural hurdles in the city council, and it was not formally offered to O'Malley until October 1957.

Back during the previous May (months before the Dodgers' case was settled), the Giants had announced that they were leaving for San Francisco. O'Malley had indeed talked Horace Stoneham into moving to California, but he had not persuaded the Giants owner to leave New York. Stoneham had already made that decision, but he originally planned to take the team to Minneapolis, where the Giants had a Triple A affiliate.

With the Dodgers finally in Los Angeles, O'Malley faced the question of where they would play. Just a month before spring training, the Rose Bowl and Wrigley Field were being considered for the 1958 season. Even more threatening was the news that the city's contract with the Dodgers to provide land for the new stadium would be reviewed by the voters of the county in a ballot referendum in June 1958.

The referendum was narrowly passed, approving the contract, but then a local court invalidated the agreement in a taxpayer suit. That decision was not reversed by the California state supreme court until January 1959, long after O'Malley had expected to break ground at Chavez Ravine.

Dodger Stadium opened in 1962, and it has been the gold mine of major league baseball ever since. Attendance records have been routinely set and broken, and Dodgers baseball has been a virtual license to print money. This Midas touch in the hills of Southern California has fueled the bitter insistence of Brooklynites that O'Malley had it planned all along.

While the Dodgers' move is a dark myth in the pubs of Brooklyn, it represents a different fable in some of the front offices of baseball. The Los Angeles market has been seen as a kind of El Dorado, a gold mine that pours wealth into its owners' pockets with little effort. The O'Malleys have been respected as talented and serious businessmen, but there is an element in many appraisals of the Dodgers' success that suggests their riches were inevitable.

The El Dorado mystique has become an important aspect of selecting baseball markets, but the record of major league baseball in California is strong support for the proposition that the Dodgers' success was not a sure thing. The Angels, even with Gene Autry's money, had to abandon Los Angeles for Orange County to find their niche. San Diego nearly lost the Padres, the Athletics have had some lean years in Oakland, and the Giants are likely to move from San Francisco.

The fiction of El Dorado is one of the unfortunate conclusions that have misled fans, owners, and public officials to make serious errors in understanding the formula for a successful baseball franchise. A more accurate perspective would note that first, while O'Malley was certainly looking out for his best interests, he understood them differently than today's owners do. He saw the advantages of owning his own stadium, and he rejected the public stadium that has since become so prevalent. The Dodgers' move, in hindsight, was poorly prepared; effort and luck rescued O'Malley from what was a careless and potentially disastrous move.

Second, public officials should not cave in to demands from club owners to throw the public treasury at a franchise. Los Angeles's public officials negotiated a reasonable deal with the Dodgers, and local residents then scrutinized the agreement both at the ballot box and in court. The pot of gold that Walter O'Malley found in Los Angeles was not thrust upon him; it was inspired in part by the lack of guarantees from the local government, the very guarantees that so many other cities lavish on their clubs.

Finally, these apparently esoteric considerations of public finance and decision-making procedures are generally more significant than an owner's personality. The institutional factors are more obscure and less titillating, but they are neglected at the community's peril.

* * *

In our litigious age, it is conceivable that franchise moves are a thing of the past. No club has transferred in the past twenty years, and even the Giants are trying to stay in the Bay Area when they finally escape Candlestick. Baseball's peripatetic age may have passed, but what is far more common now is the *threat* to move. This ploy has extracted enormous concessions from municipal and state governments.

In the years since the Dodgers and the Giants left, New York has put itself in a corner trying to keep the Yankees. During the 1970s, the John Lindsay administration agreed to spend $20 million to renovate Yankee Stadium and secure the Yankees into the twenty-first century.

That decision was reached because the Yankees were owned at the time by the Columbia Broadcasting System, whose chairman, William S. Paley, had decided to sell the club. Paley preferred to sell to someone who would keep the Yankees in New York, but complicating the transaction was the condition of Yankee Stadium. The old park needed major repairs, and their cost on top of the purchase price for the Yankees might have made it easier to deal with an out-of-town buyer.

Norman Redlich was an assistant corporation counsel at the time and the man whom Lindsay charged with renovating Yankee Stadium.[6] The administration decided to become involved in the Yankees' case because of rumors that the club would move to New Orleans or the New Jersey Meadowlands if the stadium problem could not be fixed.

Redlich does not remember Lindsay as a great baseball fan, but the mayor feared the impact on the city if the Yankees moved. The same urban renewal powers that Robert Moses had declined to use to keep the Dodgers in Brooklyn were used in the 1970s to keep the Yankees in the South Bronx. The stadium itself was owned by the Knights of Columbus, and the land was owned by Rice University. Both properties were condemned without serious opposition. They were taken by the city, with the former owners compensated for their losses.

The expected costs of renovation were given as $24 million, a number somewhat pulled out of the air because it was the tab for the construction of Shea Stadium ten years earlier. The final cost for the stadium itself was $57 million, with about twice that sum spent in the neighborhood for parking and roads.

The higher costs would have been a problem under any circumstances, but given the times, they were a disaster. The contracts were all signed well before renovation began in 1973, and Moody's raised the city's credit rating that year. But as the stadium reopened two years later, New York was in the grip of a fiscal crisis that put the most essential services in jeopardy.

During that same period, the Yankees were sold to a group headed by George Steinbrenner for $12 million, and there the irony begins. The public control of the stadium was supposed to secure the Yankees in the South Bronx, but Steinbrenner threatened to break the current lease on the grounds that the city and the state had failed to meet their obligations. Negotiations on a new lease have since broken down, and the speculation that the Yankees will move is again rife.

The premise that no buyer would have wanted to pay for the Yankees and the stadium may have been true in the 1970s. But in hindsight, the club that was purchased for $12 million is now worth probably well over $200 million in the market, and if the private ownership of a renovated stadium were added to the assets, the value would be even more enormous.

As things stand, Bronx borough president Fernando Ferrer presides over a community whose reputation is synonymous with urban disaster.[7] Despite a number of prosperous and even magnificent neighborhoods, the Bronx is associated with drugs, violence, and despair. The public subsidy that renovated Yankee Stadium in the 1970s did little if anything to forestall the problems that today seem to paralyze the Bronx,

Portable Franchises

yet Fernando Ferrer now proposes replacing Yankee Stadium with a $200-million facility in another part of the Bronx.

The suggestion was made during the first few weeks of David Dinkins's mayoralty amid news of higher taxes and reduced services. On the face of it, the idea is another indication of misplaced priorities and fiscal insanity, but Ferrer offers a cogent explanation of how the stadium issue looks from his perspective inside the Bronx courthouse made infamous by Tom Wolfe in *The Bonfire of the Vanities*.

The thought of losing the Yankees is repugnant to Ferrer. He sees that prospect not only in symbolic terms, what he calls a perception that New York is "bleeding," but also as a financial matter—what the effect would be on the city's bond rating, what other nervous companies within the Bronx might do. Whether people should attach so much importance to a baseball team is a luxurious question to a politician who is convinced that such importance *does* attach to the Yankees.

Ferrer's problem is a wonderful opportunity to politicians elsewhere, especially in the state of New Jersey, which has coveted the Yankees for years. The Meadowlands Complex drew both of New York City's pro football teams to Giants Stadium. The New Jersey Nets of the NBA and the Devils of the NHL play in the Brendan Byrne Arena. And most important for the state's treasury, the ponies run at the Meadowlands Raceway, paying for all the above.

Governor Jim Florio has actively courted the Yankees to induce them to cross the Hudson River and join the festivities in the Meadowlands. One stadium proposal was rejected by the state electorate, but other plans are routinely floated with a variety of funding techniques.

Back in the Bronx, Ferrer considers how he can keep the Yankees from the clutches of Florio, a fellow Democrat, and he ponders what the Yankees are looking for when their lease expires in a little more than ten years. He estimates that the necessary improvements to Yankee Stadium would cost between $120 and $140 million.

Operating under the assumption that the Yankees must be kept in New York to avoid the economic and psychological damage that a move could cause, and because keeping the Yankees where they are now would run well over $100 million, Ferrer asks how much more it would cost to simply build a new stadium in a more hospitable part of the Bronx.

If for $200 million he could build a facility by the Whitestone Bridge in the southeast corner of the Bronx, the Yankees could draw crowds more easily from Long Island, and they could keep their base support in New York City and Westchester County. Correcting what he sees as the principal flaw of the last agreement, Ferrer would want the Yankees to sign a fifty-year lease.

From the beleaguered perspective of his office, what Ferrer proposes makes some sense. Under the terms of the franchise relocation game, some community will be likely to give the Yankees what the team is pursuing, so can New York fail to match the best available offer? This dilemma represents the link between portable franchises and the stadium game.

New York does not have a monopoly on unstable franchises and difficult stadium choices. The White Sox raised to an art form the threat to move as they bargained for a replacement for Comiskey Park. Governor Jim Thompson feverishly worked the Illinois state legislature for approval of a new stadium that would keep the Sox in Chicago. A midnight deadline was averted by the old practice of stopping the clock before the stroke of twelve, and the threatened move to St. Petersburg was prevented.

The extraordinary political activity in Illinois salvaged a franchise that was certain to move to Florida. Bill Johnson of the Florida Progress Corporation worked on bringing the White Sox to St. Petersburg, and he says that at one point the move was a sure thing.[8] He says that the intervention of Governor Thompson and the Illinois legislature reversed a decision that had been set.

Johnson adds that he is satisfied that the Sox owners Eddie

Einhorn and Jerry Reinsdorf did not play Illinois and Florida against each other. He displays no bitterness about the failure of his city to secure the club, stating simply that Reinsdorf and Einhorn understand the business of running sports teams.

That business has been practiced differently in San Francisco, where the Giants also have looked for a new home, because of their dissatisfaction with Candlestick Park. In contrast with the White Sox, the Giants have tried to stay in the neighborhood.[9] Their proposed moves have been to San Jose and Santa Clara, cities immediately to the south of the Bay Area.

Voters of San Francisco have had several opportunities to approve a new stadium for the Giants, and they have rejected the proposals. To the Giants' chagrin, the team has not received more enthusiastic attention in the suburbs. Santa Clara most recently turned down the opportunity to build a new stadium.

As this is written, the Giants are on the ballot again. The voters of San Jose will decide if they want to increase their utility taxes to finance the lion's share of a new stadium. The electorate will have the chance in a public campaign to decide if the history of such stadiums warrants their support and their money. One must approve of this process that puts the decision in the hands of those who will bear the financial burden; previous stadium votes in the Bay Area suggest that those voters can examine the merits of this issue with a clearer eye than most public officials in America.

Inevitably, the trauma of losing a franchise raises the political stakes of franchise moves. The real and imagined economic and emotional costs suffered by the abandoned community inspire proposals for federal legislation, and bills were introduced in the early 1980s to restrict owners from moving their clubs as they please. The immediate inspiration for these bills was the case of the Raiders of the National Football League.

Like Bill Veeck, Al Davis was a maverick among his fellow

owners. Like Veeck, his attempt to move his team to a more lucrative market was rebuffed by his colleagues. Unlike Veeck, Davis moved the Raiders anyway. Davis's defiance was upheld in federal courts, and the power of the National Football League to restrict the transfer of its teams was curtailed.

A subsequent football move that has affected baseball was the abandonment of Baltimore by Robert Irsay, owner of the Baltimore Colts. His midnight escape to Indianapolis while still negotiating a new stadium agreement made a strong impression on public officials in Maryland and influenced their negotiations with the Orioles on a new stadium.

Baseball enjoys a broader antitrust immunity than does football, so conceivably the major leagues would have greater power over individual franchises than the NFL did over the Raiders and the Colts. No baseball team has threatened to move without league approval, but the proposed governmental restrictions would apply to baseball as well as every other professional sport.

The several versions of the franchise restriction bills had the common features of requiring a club to demonstrate that it was losing money with few prospects for reversing that trend, that a stadium was inadequate, or that terms of a lease agreement had not been met.

This legislative strategy for securing teams in their communities is inherently flawed. First, the financial losses are difficult to evaluate. A club may have operating losses year after year, but the equity of the franchise could climb at an even higher rate. The operating losses may reflect poor management rather than indifferent fans, indicating that some club executives should relocate—but not the entire team.

Baseball clubs have been stable in their markets for twenty years, but the threat to move remains credible. The only impediment is the fraternity of fellow owners, who must decide if the proposed move is in the best interests of the game. The only time the baseball owners have rejected a move was when Bill Veeck was involved. With Veeck gone from the scene, what restrictions remain? The government may be unable to prevent the reckless transfer of a ball club, and the league may be unwilling. How then can a community hope to keep a franchise home? The answer can be found in the self-interest of the owners: tie them financially to the community through the ownership of the ball park, the only significant fixed asset in baseball.

NOTES

1. Bogue, *Population of the United States*, p. 120.
2. For an analysis of these measures, see Arthur T. Johnson, "Municipal Administration and the Sports Franchise Relocation Issue," *Public Administration Review* 43, no.6 (November–December 1983).
3. Veeck, *Veeck as in Wreck*.
4. Bavasi interview.
5. See Neil Sullivan, *The Dodgers Move West* (New York: Oxford University Press, 1987).
6. Norman Redlich, interview, Redlich's office, March 12, 1991.
7. Fernando Ferrer, interview, Ferrer's office, September 6, 1991.
8. Bill Johnson, interview by telephone, June 10, 1991.
9. Corey Busch, interview, Busch's office, August 23, 1990.

4

Playgrounds
of the Rich

They are described as "emerald cathedrals," and they take life
in the imagination of a fictional Iowa farmer in *Field of
Dreams*. But in reality, stadiums are the principal capital investment of major league franchises, and when we fans become too deluded with the romance of baseball—when we
forget who really owns the team—we get stuck with the bill
for that investment.

Virtually every change in the business of baseball since
World War II has diminished the power and status of the
major league owners. No one grovels to the owners any-
more—with one exception: Elected officials across the country have fallen all over themselves to open the public purse to
build stadiums that by every reasonable standard should have
been paid for by the ball clubs that use them.

Stadiums have been built by cities to attract new teams
and to keep old ones. A number of communities and their
political leaders have resisted this impulse, but very few
people in baseball believe any longer that clubs themselves should pay for their own stadiums. During an era of
tax revolts and deep suspicion about anything done by government, some cities and states have sunk enormous
amounts of money to the direct benefit of owners who are

wealthy enough to finance some kind of new stadium privately.

During the 1960s and 1970s, the old ball parks of the World War I era were abandoned as if they were on fire. Sixteen new stadiums were built at public expense during those two decades, some of them attractive, others awful. Now another spate of construction is under way, as perfectly adequate facilities are dismissed as unacceptable. What are the lessons of the stadium game, and how well have we learned them?

Suburban growth doomed the old neighborhood park that could be reached by foot, trolley, bus, or subway. By the 1950s, the automobile had to be accommodated. Not only did cars require adequate parking, but they also needed spacious roadways. The park that was tucked amid narrow meandering streets was asking for obliteration.

During the 1950s, virtually every one of the sixteen major league teams played in an old neighborhood park. Now only Fenway Park and Wrigley Field can be expected to endure for the foreseeable future, and that judgment may be optimistic. Tiger Stadium will likely follow Comiskey Park into oblivion. Yankee Stadium has been renovated once, but it may be abandoned in another decade.

The old parks are vital to the middle-aged fan's memories of the postwar game because the parts were so distinctive. If we followed a club in those years, we can easily bring the team to mind today because its field of play was so striking. The replacement stadiums of the 1960s and 1970s have been, for the most part, uniform utilitarian mediocrities.

By comparison, Ebbets Field has been transformed in memory to something like the cathedral at Chartres. The Polo Grounds was clearly less elegant, but as the place where Willie roamed it was accorded a special grace in its late years.

Cincinnati's Crosley Field included a left field that sloped upward to the fence, and the center-field wall displayed a challenging message for the umpires: Batted Ball Hitting Concrete Wall on Fly to Right of White Line—Home Run.

Forbes Field was located next to the University of Pittsburgh, and the site eventually became part of the Pitt campus. The park was noted for an enormous center field, the fence looming 457 feet from home plate; a backstop far enough behind the plate to turn Joe Garagiola into a distance runner; and lovely trees beyond the outfield walls. The distance to left field was shortened to help Ralph Kiner, who needed little assistance, and a screen was periodically raised to protect the right-field stands that were a mere 300 feet away.

A similar screen was erected in right field at Sportsman's Park in St. Louis. The foul pole was 310 feet from the plate, and, when the screen was used, it extended 156 feet toward center field to augment a power alley that was only 350 feet.

It is doubtful that any screen could have kept one of Mickey Mantle's home runs in Griffith Stadium in Washington, D.C. Mantle's reputation as a power hitter became legendary on April 17, 1953, when he cleared the left-field wall, a city street, and a three-story tenement. The blast was estimated at 565 feet. Bowie Kuhn's introduction to baseball was as a scoreboard boy at Griffith Stadium, and Marvin Miller probably believes he should have stayed right there.

Connie Mack Stadium was home to both the Phillies and the Athletics. It was the first modern stadium when it opened in 1909. Its steel and concrete was a radical break from the wooden grandstands that had contributed to a number of dangerous fires in baseball's early years. This neighborhood park survived until 1970, when its elegance was abandoned for the multipurpose Veterans Stadium.

The old Comiskey Park was the oldest in the country when it last served during the 1990 season. It was an antique that did not appeal to everyone's taste, and it was a poor relation in a town that also has the "friendly confines" of Wrigley Field. But Comiskey, if not charming, was a relic with character, and some fans were utterly devoted to the park.

All these ball parks are now gone, and we properly remember them as something special. But they also included characteristics that were annoying and even dangerous. Pillars obstructed fans' views, and the sight lines might not have been well planned. Unforgiving fences ruined the careers of several aggressive outfielders. None of the parks was originally designed for night baseball or automobile traffic. And the press facilities might not have had adequate room for television. We might think we would not care about these things now, but that may be just the nostalgia talking.

When the Boston Braves migrated to Milwaukee in 1953, they not only broke the old alignment of teams, but they also introduced a new relationship between a franchise and its city. For the first time, a municipal government became a direct partner in baseball by financing the construction of the team's stadium.

Following the Ray Kinsella *Field of Dreams* strategy, Milwaukee broke ground for County Stadium in 1950, and the Braves came. The facility was financed through pension funds of county employees, and the stadium was then leased to the Braves. The club was freed of maintenance expenses and split parking and concessions with the county.

County Stadium was no breakthrough in design, but it did provide a generous amount of parking. In their new home, the Braves reversed their financial fortunes dramatically, making more money in their first home stand than they had during the entire 1952 season in Boston. A terrific young ball club and a city that had been starved for major league play were more important factors in the Braves' prosperity than the ball park, but County Stadium compared very favorably with the cramped facilities in declining neighborhoods that characterized the conditions where many other teams played.

Baltimore and Kansas City followed similar strategies in luring the Orioles and the Athletics, respectively. Minor league parks were purchased by local governments and upgraded to major league standards. Leases were then negotiated with a relocating major league club covering rent, maintenance, parking, and concessions.

The first modern stadium of the postwar era was the disaster of San Francisco, Candlestick Park. The stadium was rushed to completion for the 1960 season amid every aggravation associated with public construction projects. Strikes, lawsuits, allegations of corruption, and grand jury probes threatened the stadium. Alas, the problems were overcome. The Giants and the rest of the league learned again the lesson that the three most important factors in real estate are location, location, location.

Candlestick has been renovated several times. The natural turf was replaced with a synthetic field that in turn was replaced with natural turf. The outer walls of the park were extended until they enclosed the field, helping curtail the notorious winds. Withal, the place remains impossible for baseball. One of the Giants' problems is meteorological. The weather in San Francisco is better for baseball during the autumn. The summer game in the Bay Area should be football.

Thirty years after the Giants' new era began with fog and wind, the team is patiently waiting to relocate to a more hospitable site. Candlestick will remain an adequate place for the 49ers, but it will likely always be baseball's version of the Edsel.

At the time the Giants were hurtling toward a fiasco, the Dodgers were negotiating a maze of legal and political challenges to build the one successful stadium of its time. Walter O'Malley saw the Braves' turnaround in Milwaukee and concluded almost immediately that Ebbets Field was doomed. The Brooklyn park would require increased maintenance, all borne by the club, and as Brooklynites moved to the suburbs, the trek to Ebbets Field and its 700 parking places would become less appealing.

The Dodgers were the leading money maker in the National League during the 1950s, but that was a result primarily of their broadcast revenues. The gate was still the key to prosperity in the 1950s, and in that area the Dodgers were far behind the Braves. In the mid-1950s, Milwaukee made about a million dollars more a year from attendance than did Brooklyn. For 1955, the Braves took in $2,556,410 to the Dodgers' $1,549,062, and the following year the Braves made $2,603,354 from attendance, while the Dodgers took in $1,790,275.[1] The Dodgers' gate receipts were ahead of the other National League clubs, but Milwaukee was taking the game to a new level of prosperity, and Walter O'Malley was not about to let the Braves get there alone.

O'Malley was uninterested in playing in a public facility like County Stadium, but he saw that the Braves were positioned to make potentially more money than the Dodgers despite the differences in market size. The Braves' first seasons of two million attendance for the National League confirmed O'Malley's fears. The Dodgers' pursuit of a new stadium to compete with the Braves would lead them 3,000 miles from the streets of Flatbush.

The Dodgers owner received a crash course in California politics, beginning with his arrival at the airport, where a clerk informed him that his agreement with the city and county would be placed on the June 1958 county ballot as a referendum. That delay, as well as some ensuing court cases, were costly to O'Malley, but the Dodgers owner kept his eye on the stadium at Chavez Ravine as a vindication of his struggles in New York and a testament to himself and his family.

A stark departure from the financing of other modern stadiums, Dodger Stadium was paid for with private money. In a remarkably simple venture, O'Malley put several million dollars of his own money into the stadium and then secured a loan from the Bank of America for the balance.[2] The B of A had originally been one of three California banks that were to advance O'Malley $5 million apiece, but the other two banks withdrew from the plan. Undeterred, B of A offered to lend O'Malley the entire $15 million, and he was again rescued from possible disaster.

The Dodgers president covered himself with a ten-year advertising deal with the Union Oil Company that guaranteed the revenues that could repay the bank loan. If the Dodgers had been a bust in Los Angeles, O'Malley would not have been destitute, but his stadium deal remains notable because it puts the burden to produce where it belongs—on the club owner.

A bank loan would not be the financial instrument for stadium financing today, but the more important point about Dodger Stadium is that Walter O'Malley, rather than the community, was on the hook. If great profits were to be made, they were properly his, and if losses occurred, they would have been O'Malley's problem rather than the city's. The financial instrument for stadium construction may now be more sophisticated, but the political principal in the Dodger Stadium case remains sound.

Local government did play a role in building Dodger Stadium, but not the central one. The facility was not designed as a neighborhood park, so access roads from the adjacent freeways were needed. That infrastructure cost about $4 million, and it was paid for by the taxpayers. That rather negligible investment has been repaid over again through property taxes on the stadium.

Financial returns aside, what Los Angeles has received from the Chavez Ravine agreement is the most secure major league franchise in the game. Even if a financial disaster befell the Dodgers in the future, the city would be substantially insulated from the effects. The stadium would not revert to the city if the Dodgers felt compelled to move again because the fixed asset of the stadium ties the club to the community in a way that a lease never could. If the Dodgers were to be sold, the stadium would likely be part of the deal, thereby keeping the team in the city regardless of the future decisions of the O'Malley family. And if the scenario of another Dodgers move seems preposterous, remember that the Yankees may very well leave New York even though they enjoy revenues far beyond those of the Dodgers.

Without a doubt, Dodger Stadium has been the gold mine of baseball, but the reason behind the wealth may not be properly understood. Irving Kristol, the neoconservative social critic, has observed that the Horatio Alger myths insisted on a point that modern American business sometimes forgets.[3] In those rags-to-riches stories, the abundance that the hero ultimately enjoyed was not the focus of his pursuits. Rather, the goal was to work hard to offer a high-quality product or service at a fair price. The figures in Alger's stories who chased money for its own sake were never the heroes of his tales; rather, the people who were admirable became wealthy as a result of their diligence and persistence in providing something that benefited the community.

Without proposing Walter O'Malley for canonization, Dodger Stadium was built to be the best possible facility to present baseball to the fans of Southern California. Millions have poured in to the Dodgers because that objective continues to be met. Both Walter and Peter O'Malley bypassed the humble origins of the Horatio Alger stories, but they have increased the family treasury through strict attention to the lessons of that myth.

If money alone were the purpose of Dodger Stadium, three obvious sources of wealth could be cashed in at any time. First, luxury boxes could be added. The franchise caps its season tickets at 27,000, so imagine what could be charged for corporate comfort. A dozen season tickets currently gross less than $15,000 for the Dodgers. By packaging those seats in a luxury box, perhaps ten times that amount could be charged.

Second, billboards could go up next to the scoreboards and bleachers. The small Union Oil "76" emblems leave plenty of room for beer and cigarette signs. The strategic positioning of those ads for camera angles would yield further revenue, as products are subtly advertised on television during the course of a game.

Finally, beyond the parking lots, the Dodgers have considerable property where hotels and office buildings could be constructed. Peter O'Malley says that he receives brief inquiries about such projects from time to time, but he has shown no serious interest in them.

Dodger Stadium is maintained as it was built—as arguably the finest facility in baseball. The money flows from that commitment, and that is simply good business—Horatio Alger would approve.

Comparing other franchises with the Dodgers has very limited utility. Not only is the Los Angeles market larger than any but New York, but the team and the stadium are owned free and clear, removing the debt that burdens some other clubs. The O'Malleys, through skill and luck, are the only family to have operated its club successfully into a fifth decade without the benefit of an outside business, and one of the primary reasons for that record is that Walter O'Malley made a wise decision in building Dodger Stadium.

Consider the fate of the four other teams that moved during the 1950s. The Athletics and the Braves have already moved again, the Giants are considering a move out of San Francisco, and the Orioles seriously threatened to move a few years ago.

More to the point, consider the five stadiums associated with those teams in relation to the franchise's stability. Municipal Stadium in Kansas City hosted the Athletics from 1955 through 1967. Voters had approved a bond to build a new public stadium, but Charlie Finley saw greener pastures in Oakland. When the Royals arrived in 1969, they played in Municipal Stadium until the new facility, Royals Stadium, was ready in 1973. As a public investment, Municipal Stadium in Kansas City had very limited utility. Its twelve years of major league service were not even as long as George Brett's career.

Playgrounds of the Rich

Memorial Stadium in Baltimore was dedicated "as a memorial to all those who so valiantly fought and served in the World Wars with eternal gratitude to those who made the supreme sacrifice to preserve equality and freedom throughout the world." The gratitude may be eternal, but the stadium secured the Orioles only from 1954 through 1991.

If one were to pick the baseball stadium that most deserves to be abandoned, Memorial Stadium would not be it. The park has its problems. An Orioles game requires a drive through narrow neighborhood streets, and parking at the stadium itself is limited. The passageways at the stadium are somewhat narrow. The food stands are pedestrian. The upper deck is a ski jumper's delight, and some of the views are obstructed. But the facility is clean, and its modest appearance and design make complaints about its shortcomings seem rather pretentious. How grand does a ball park have to be?

The Orioles owners, including the late Edward Bennett Williams, realized that Memorial Stadium could not generate the revenues of more modern facilities. As a postwar stadium, Memorial lacked the luxury boxes, the accommodation to television, the training facilities, easy access for fans, and elaborate food concessions that have become essential in the minds of the fans, players, and owners.

A new stadium was not one of the community's crying concerns, and Baltimore voters rejected a measure that called for public financing of a new park. Mayor William Schaefer pressed for a public stadium despite his constituents' expressed wishes, and, traumatized by the midnight flight of the Baltimore Colts, Maryland officials agreed to replace the stadium with a more accessible ball park. Still in good repair, Memorial Stadium will be a relic at the age of thirty-seven.

Orioles Park at Camden Yards introduces a new era in stadium construction by reintroducing the design of the old neighborhood parks. The new ball park affords a charming place to see a game, and, not incidentally, boosts the value of the Orioles franchise. Taking advantage of that windfall, Eli

83

Jacobs has the club on the market. After a public investment that the voters had tried to reject, the principal beneficiary of the new ball park is the owner, who can pocket millions in profits after risking none of his own money in the new facility. If an unflattering article in *Business Week* is accurate, the public largesse that Eli Jacobs has received in Baltimore will make the Orioles a rare profitable venture for him.[4]

County Stadium was home to the Braves on their thirteen-year visit to Milwaukee, and it has served the Brewers since their migration from Seattle. The park is similar in design to Memorial Stadium, both of them belonging to the same era. County Stadium is relatively easy to reach because it is located next to an expressway, and parking is plentiful. The stadium is now under the gun as the Brewers seek to replicate the Dodgers model with a privately financed stadium in Milwaukee. Unlike the Orioles, Bud Selig has scrupulously avoided any threats to move the team, but the implication would have to be apparent to any public official who is familiar with the history of franchises and their communities.

As with Dodger Stadium, the attempt to build a private stadium may be more difficult than simply allowing the state to do the job. Selig has endured many of the trials that Walter O'Malley faced in trying to secure the limited assistance that he needs from city and county officials in Milwaukee. William Schaefer and Jim Thompson jumped through hoops in Maryland and Illinois to give stadiums to the Orioles and White Sox, but stricter scrutiny is the order of the day in Wisconsin. Selig may need a touch of the O'Malley luck to prevail in Milwaukee.

What accounts for the exceptional history of Dodger Stadium, the sole success of the early replacement stadiums? The blanket ideological belief that anything done by private business is superior to anything done by government is not much better than the El Dorado myth or the devil theory that sees the Dodgers' success as an evil design. But in this case, credible evidence suggests that government should forswear the construction of ball parks.

84

Playgrounds of the Rich

Municipal, Memorial, and County stadiums reflected designs as uninspiring as their names. At best, such facilities are functional, but they add little value to the franchise. Attendance will rest almost entirely on how the team plays and on how well the club is marketed. Stadiums can attract additional fans if they are pleasant places to visit (and that quality can help a club sustain a fan base through the inevitable lean years), but few public stadiums are pleasant enough to draw fans for the architectural appeal.

If there truly is a spiritual quality to a baseball stadium, it may be that the facility can hold the ghosts of past teams. A fan can sense that great players and games graced the park years ago. Some people get that eternal feeling in a redwood forest, others in an architectural ruin. Baseball fans can capture that moment in some of the stadiums that were built with a reverence for the game.

The transcendent aspect of some stadiums is very different from the mawkish sentimentality that is often invoked when hustling the public into paying for a new ball park. The critical distinction is a sense of proportion: a healthy appreciation for the gifts of baseball does not need to extend to a desperate "Keep the team at any cost!" panic that squanders the resources of a city on a privileged few.

Few communities saw that Dodger Stadium worked not so much because it was new but because Walter O'Malley had put his own money on the line. The novelty of the stadium was its most salient feature, and suddenly having a new stadium became the fashion in baseball. The limitations of the old ball parks, borne patiently for years, were now intolerable. The new stadiums in California exposed the old parks as relics of a bygone era at a time when being mod was everything that mattered.

During the fifteen years after Dodger Stadium opened, thirteen more stadiums were built for major league baseball. None was privately financed, and the deficiencies of a political ball park began to become apparent in their design. The new parks were not simply pedestrian like those of the mid-1950s; rather, for the most part, they were egregiously ugly.

Shea Stadium (1964) looks unfinished a quarter of a century after it opened, and its location by LaGuardia Airport has distracted both players and fans when flight patterns direct jets over second base. Shea was designed primarily for baseball, with the New York Jets wedged into the stadium until they departed to New Jersey. One has a sense that Dodger Stadium might have inspired the design for Shea; unfortunately, the inspiration did not translate into elegance.

The Astrodome (1965) was astounding as the first stadium to put the game indoors. At the time, the domed roof was such a marvel that few challenged its description as the Eighth Wonder of the World. When natural grass had to be replaced with the synthetic replica known as Astroturf, the adjustment seemed to fit such an exotic stadium, and few protests ensued. Why complain? How many domed stadiums would there be? And without a dome, who would have any use for plastic grass?

Atlanta–Fulton County Stadium, Busch Stadium in St. Louis, and Anaheim Stadium all opened in 1966. The first two were open-air facilities employing the doughnut shape that the Astrodome had introduced. That design accommodated the NFL franchises that both of those cities had, and since the public was now in the construction business, why build two stadiums when one would do? And with a football team tearing up the turf during the stretch drive of a pennant race, another rationale for plastic grass was discovered.

Busch Stadium was eventually purchased by a foundation of Anheuser-Busch, so it is privately maintained. It was the first open-air stadium to use Astroturf because, as Cardinals president Fred Kuhlman contends, the St. Louis summers are too severe to maintain an adequate grass field. That point is challenged by some agronomists, who argue that with proper maintenance, the real thing functions just fine.

Despite the widely held belief that artificial turf contributes to player injuries, the Players Association has never considered the issue of turf in negotiations with the owners.[5] Donald Fehr says he is unpersuaded that a connection between the playing surface and injuries has been established, despite the anecdotal evidence of players like Andre Dawson. Fehr also mentions that there is no drumbeat among the players to get rid of the artificial surfaces. More to the point, Fehr notes that many players have fashioned their games to the rug, so restoring real grass to every park might cost some players their livelihoods.

Anaheim Stadium, the Big A, was built for baseball, and it provided an escape from Dodger Stadium for the Angels. Their owner, Gene Autry, was outmatched in his tenant's role by his landlord, Walter O'Malley. Despite the size of Los Angeles, the Dodgers had so established themselves that the Angels needed to escape to nearby Orange County to develop their own market.

When the Rams of the NFL left Los Angeles because of their dissatisfaction with the Coliseum, the Big A was renovated for football. A dramatic A-frame scoreboard behind the left-field fence was nearly obliterated by new seats, and in appearance Anaheim Stadium resembled Candlestick South.

The Oakland–Alameda County Coliseum opened for baseball in 1968, when the A's arrived from Kansas City. It had been home to the Raiders of the NFL, but when Al Davis took the Raiders to Los Angeles, the Coliseum became a baseball-only facility. Reflecting a health-conscious California, the Oakland Coliseum is the first park in the game where cigarette smoking has been restricted to designated areas.

Jack Murphy Stadium in San Diego was also built before major league baseball arrived. The horseshoe-shaped stadium opened in 1967 and hosted the Chargers of the NFL and the Padres of the Pacific Coast League, before the National League expanded to the city in 1969.

All the California stadiums are open air with grass fields, but plastic grass returned with the doughnut design in the construction of Riverfront Stadium in Cincinnati and Three Rivers Stadium in Pittsburgh in 1970. During the following season, Veterans Stadium opened in Philadelphia. Only someone with a discerning eye for the mundane could easily distinguish the three.

Public financing and plastic grass were employed with as much grace as possible in the construction of Royals Stadium, which opened in 1973. The city fathers of Kansas City decided that expediency was not everything, and they provided separate stadiums for the Royals and the NFL's Chiefs. Real grass could elevate Royals Stadium to the heights of baseball architecture.

The next phase of stadium construction is as bad as things get. The Kingdome in Seattle opened in 1977, as did Olympic Stadium in Montreal. No argument that the weather is occasionally unpleasant for watching baseball in those cities. But minor league baseball thrived in both places for virtually the entire history of organized baseball, and neither the Seattle Mariners nor the Montreal Royals needed facilities that call to mind jai alai frontons. Domeball also arrived in Minnesota in 1982 with the Hubert H. Humphrey Metrodome, where the Twins have enjoyed a lopsided advantage in postseason play.

Toronto's Skydome is the most recent of the domed facilities. This spectacular facility has disdained the spare and functional in favor of a grand structure that includes a retractable roof, adjacent malls, and a hotel that has spiced a few Blue Jays games with some erotic scenes from rooms beyond center field.

The appeals of voyeurism aside, the Blue Jays have become the new attendance champions of major league baseball in their new home. They became the first team to have an official attendance of more than four million in a season. (The American League counts attendance by ticket sales, whereas the National League counts the bodies that pass through the turnstiles, so this mark has undoubtedly been passed in Los Angeles.) But the lesson from the Blue Jays' stadium is that if domes and plastic grass are going to be used—go all out.

A cautionary note for the Toronto franchise might be found in Houston. When the Astrodome opened in 1965, more than two million turned out to watch a ninth-place expansion team. The Astros have reached two million only one other year since, a division-winning season in 1980. The fascination with an unusual stadium may not hold up if the club is not winning.

At this point, the ball park in Toronto is a financial success, but the hotels, stores, and other ancillary services have yet to show a profit. That may happen at some point, but there is reason for concern if the project is showing a loss when the novelty still draws some fans. The grand design of Skydome seems to fit better with the fashions of the 1970s rather than the return to an intimate neighborhood style that informs most modern stadium design.

Caution and even skepticism are healthy attitudes when the public is asked to finance modern stadiums. Twenty new facilities have opened for major league baseball between 1953 and 1990. Five of them, one-fourth, have been or soon will be abandoned by the franchise. Another four—the Astrodome, Three Rivers, the Kingdome, and Olympic Stadium—house teams that at one point or another have been rumored to be heading out of town. And most of the rest have drawn crowds in spite of an antiseptic setting.

Sometimes lost in the enthusiasm about the new stadiums is that, during the 1960s, one of the targets of progress was Fenway Park. The Greater Boston Stadium Authority proposed in 1962 that a domed stadium be built for the Red Sox and the Patriots. The stadium would have been part of a complex that would have provided a new arena for the Celtics and the Bruins, but the Massachusetts legislature balked at the $90 million price tag. The proposal has been made again, perhaps as a device to draw some public money into a renovation of Fenway.

THE DIAMOND REVOLUTION

* * *

While the new stadiums have been bitter pills for many middle-age fans, some clubs now recognize that deferring to nostalgia can be good business. Stadium architects have begun to rescue the charms of the old neighborhood parks while incorporating the safety and conveniences that players and fans have come to expect.

Janet Marie Smith is directing the building of the Orioles' new stadium in Baltimore, and she explains the thinking behind the contemporary designs.[6] According to Smith, the old neighborhood stadiums were not deficient in appearance; they provided an intimacy for the fans and a layout that enhanced the game. The newer doughnut stadiums abandoned those charms.

The major problem for the old parks was their location, an improvement that the newer stadiums generally got right. The ideal for the next generation of stadiums is to take the old designs, refine them for the modern fan, and then place the ball park in a convenient setting.

Smith is optimistic about the new ball parks because they combine attractiveness with utility. Sight lines, camera angles, food concessions, and parking are far better than what can be offered at Fenway or Wrigley Field. Yet the fan will have the feeling of being at a ball park designed for baseball rather than at a stadium that conforms to the competing demands of several sports and governmental bodies.

Another vestige of the neighborhood park that will return is the smaller capacity. Despite drawing World Series crowds of greater that 90,000 in the Los Angeles Coliseum, Walter O'Malley understood that a cavernous stadium could actually cut attendance because fans would know that they could always get a seat at the last minute, so the capacity of Dodger Stadium was held to 56,000. Indeed, one of the many problems plaguing the Cleveland Indians is the 74,483 capacity at Municipal Stadium. The new ball parks will have a capacity in the low 40,000s to enhance the intimate feeling of the park and to put a little pressure on the fans to make sure that they have seats well in advance.

The new architectural designs are inspiring a rush of stadium construction that rivals that of the 1960s. The Camden Yards park opened in Baltimore for the 1992 season. The Detroit Tigers have issued a demand to local authorities to get moving on a new stadium for the Tigers. The Milwaukee Brewers have a stadium design and a site where they will build a replacement for County Stadium. The Giants are trying once more to move to San Jose. A new stadium has been approved by the voters in Cleveland. The Texas Rangers will have a new facility in a few years. And the Braves intend to move into a new facility that will be built for the Atlanta Olympics in 1996.

Other leases that will soon expire include the Mariners' in 1995, the Padres' in 2000, the Angels' in 2001, and the Yankees' in 2004. Each of those teams will be in a strong position to gain generous terms of renewal. The Suncoast Dome in Florida will be an option for any of these teams, and the threat to move will be an implicit part of negotiations between the franchises and their current cities.

With another burst of stadium construction in the country's future, fans have an interest in asking some serious questions about the next generation of ball parks. As fans we may be encouraged that the designs are more appealing than those of the 1960s and 1970s, but as citizens and taxpayers we need to insist on more than natural grass.

These stadiums are enormous investments of $100 million to $200 million or more. Who should bear that burden, and who are the principal beneficiaries of that spending?

Robert Baade, one of the top economists in the country, has considered the economic benefits of publicly financed stadiums. He has concluded that the alleged returns on this investment have been greatly exaggerated. Stadium boosters point to jobs in construction, stadium maintenance, and concessions, as well as the stimulus to the local economy from tens of thousands of people congregating regularly for the games. Baade has concluded that these claims are spurious. He writes that

> economic "growth" spurred by sports franchises or stadiums is not likely to be true growth at all, but merely "realignment." Jobs are not created, but diverted from the manufacturing economy to the service economy, or from higher-skilled to lower-skilled (and lower paid) occupations. Similarly, spending on sports activities may only divert spending from other leisure activities, and new business start-ups in the neighborhood of a stadium may be negated by business failures in other areas of the city.[7]

The advocates of public financing have been undeterred. Ralph Bolton of the Cincinnati Department of Economic Development dismissed Baade's study with the observation, "I can't see how anybody can argue that a stadium doesn't help to strengthen the center of a region. People perceive their sports team as something that belongs to all of them, and it becomes a symbol of the community."[8]

Bolton's remark is instructive for several reasons. First, it completely begs the questions that Baade addressed. Bolton insists that the "center of a region" is strengthened by a stadium. Baade has not denied that economic growth occurs in the area immediately adjacent to the stadium. His point is that the growth is based on resources that have been drawn from more peripheral areas where they could have been used more productively. The center may be strengthened by a stadium, but the spokes and rim suffer.

More to the point, whatever economic benefits may be produced by a public stadium would also result from one that is privately financed: the team would pay property taxes rather than rent, the same jobs would be needed, and the same stimulus to local commerce would be provided. The community would receive these benefits without the obligations of stadium ownership, a burden that is especially onerous if the franchise should skip town as the Braves and the Athletics did.

A second point that Bolton's objection raises is fundamentally a political one: the question of team ownership. In maintaining that people "perceive their sports team as something that belongs to all of them," Bolton has identified one of the most profound confusions in the business of sports.

The franchises, and properly their stadiums, do not belong to the fans, despite the romantic wishfulness that makes that claim. The teams belong to the people who own them. If we fans confuse ourselves with the real owners, we are ripe to be plucked. Newspapers could clarify things if they printed the standings of the O'Malley Dodgers, the Busch Cardinals, the Monaghan Tigers, et al. The cities refer only to where these private entertainment businesses are located at the moment, not to who owns them.

In traditional American capitalism, business owners have certain obligations that they must meet to be entitled to future profits. Primary among these responsibilities is that owners should risk their own capital. People in business should be sufficiently confident in their ability and work ethic to believe that they will make the investment of their own money pay off.

The public stadiums encourage a more fashionable business ethic, one that has weakened American productivity and competitiveness. In this model, one avoids risks in favor of guarantees such as golden parachutes. Executives concentrate on financial schemes rather than supplying the best product or service at the best price. Pressure to perform is eased; and if one's tepid efforts fail, one moves on—none the poorer.

What is missing from this modern ethic is a sense of stewardship, a reverence for what others have given us, along with a sense of responsibility to enrich that heritage before passing it on. If neither the past nor the future matters, then owners, players, and fans are free to act as parasites in a frenzy of the moment.

THE DIAMOND REVOLUTION

When the politics of stadium financing are confused, communities become hostage to club owners. Having committed the capital to build or to renovate a stadium, the city is in a position to be pressured by the franchise for future concessions. If the city takes a firm line against the club, the threat to relocate is eminently credible.

A lease that ties a team to a city for about a century might offer reasonable security, but the duration of leases may be moving in the other direction. The new Comiskey Park lease will hold the White Sox for twenty years, and the agreement between the Orioles and the state of Maryland is for only fifteen years.

Conversely, if the stadium were financed by the team, then it would have to stay in order for the owner to recoup the investment. If the team's owner tired of the city, her financial self-interest would likely dictate selling the team rather than trying to move it and sell the stadium. As the Baltimore case suggests, franchises may be worth much more after a city has provided the club with a new stadium, so an owner might sell and reap the profits of an investment that was provided by the public.

The potential benefits of private stadiums fuel the imagination and spin an alternative fable for the past several decades of baseball. Suppose city administrations had limited their stadium assistance to help in site acquisition and construction of the infrastructure, considerable help though far less generous than the deals that in fact were made.

An importuning owner who lobbied for a sweeter deal would have been told of the compelling needs in our cities and that neglecting crime, education, health, and transportation to further line the pockets of a club owner would be out of the question. Falling back on their own resources, the owners of the 1960s and 1970s would have likely been forced to build more modest ball parks than the multipurpose doughnuts that public construction spawned.

Many owners during the 1960s could have secured the kind of financing that Walter O'Malley received in Los Angeles. The Carpenters in Philadelphia are part of the Du Pont family. Busch in St. Louis had the brewery money. The Galbreaths in Pittsburgh were prominent in horse breeding. These owners lacked a commitment to the baseball business more than they lacked money.

A stadium design that enhanced baseball might have looked like something between Wrigley Field and Camden Yards. The heritage of baseball in Cincinnati, Pittsburgh, and Philadelphia would have been preserved in those settings rather than seriously compromised in ill-advised accommodations to the NFL.

Having invested tens of millions of dollars of their own money in a fixed asset, the owners would have been tied to the community. If they wanted to sell their team, they would have had to sell the stadium, too, so the new owners would be similarly committed to making baseball prosper in their team's present home.

With the option of moving to another city limited by the stadium investment, franchises would have appealed only to serious business executives who knew how to make the team profitable. The frivolous dilettante who wanted to dabble in a hobby could instead develop a stamp collection.

Having tied up much of their wealth in a stadium, the owners would have significantly less money for operating expenses, specifically player salaries. When free agency arrived, the owners would have bid competitively at the margin of the salary range, but the huge, sudden increases would have been more difficult to finance. Players would be millionaires instead of multimillionaires, with every other financial aspect of the business reduced commensurately.

This fantasy is dismissed by owners, commissioners, and union chiefs, each of whom benefits from the public largesse that baseball receives. Their reasons for consigning the scenario to the ivory tower vary considerably, but all conclude that publicly financed stadiums are simply the way things are. But the future of stadium financing is going to be more complicated than either the public gifts of the past or the Bank of America loan. Public-private partnerships are the emerging trend, and they take the issue of risks and benefits into an intricate array of possibilities.

Corey Busch, president of the San Francisco Giants, will have to face these new options in replacing Candlestick. When first looking for a replacement for Candlestick, the Giants intended to build their own ball park in San Jose. They were blocked in the deal by then San Francisco mayor Diane Feinstein.

By the time the Giants were able to move, the Tax Reform Act of 1986 had taken effect.[9] The legislation restricted the use of tax-exempt bonds for projects like sports facilities. Faced with the loss of tax exemption on the interest to be paid, the Giants would have had to lay out more money in interest to compensate for the lost tax advantages. The extra increment was too much for the Giants, and they decided to go with a public stadium again. Having made that adjustment, the team has yet to find a community in the Bay Area that is willing to provide a new facility. Perhaps different public-private formulas need to be examined until the right balance is struck to suit the values of the electorate in the Bay Area.

The tax exemption of bonds for stadium financing was instrumental in the building of the last privately financed sports facility: Joe Robbie Stadium in Miami. Built for the Dolphins of the NFL, the stadium will be the home of the expansion Florida Marlins. Ninety million dollars in tax-exempt bonds were sold to finance construction. The bonds were secured through ten-year leases on the stadium's luxury boxes. A public authority, a quasigovernmental institution, worked with several large banks to raise the needed funds. After the 1986 changes in the tax law, that kind of deal is no longer feasible.

Two of the new stadiums were eligible to use tax-exempt bonds because they were under way during a grace period that the law allowed. The Orioles' new stadium is financed through tax-exempt bonds that were grandfathered under the 1986 law; other taxable bonds were used to acquire the site, $35 million in money from a sports lottery was made available, and private leases of luxury suites and scoreboard advertising added more revenue.[10] And the new Comiskey Park was financed through bonds that will be retired through hotel and restaurant taxes.

One irony of the federal tax reform is that eliminating the tax benefits of private bonds can put local taxpayers even more firmly on the hook for a new stadium. Sam Katz is the leading financial adviser in the country for stadium construction, and he was the designer of the Joe Robbie financial deal. He explains the decisions to eliminate the tax exemption for private stadium bonds as part of the effort to cut the federal budget deficit.[11] But whatever benefits go to the federal government are offset by the burdens assumed by state and local governments when they assume the direct costs of stadium construction. Special taxes, dedicated to stadium construction, have been approved in some communities, thereby relieving private parties of even more financial responsibility.

The new stadium for the Cleveland Indians, for example, will be financed through a public-private partnership in which the state's half of the money will be raised through a voter-approved tax on tobacco and alcohol in Cuyahoga County. In Texas, an increase in the public utility tax will finance a new stadium for the Texas Rangers. Katz explains that these taxes are relatively small, so the public does not associate them with the normal objects of tax revolts: income and property taxes.

While the architectural design of stadiums is becoming more elegant, the financial and political aspects of stadium construction may become less accessible to the citizens who bear the responsibility for these expenditures. The public should have some kind of reasonably straightforward mechanism to decide whether its money should be committed to building these stadiums. Voters in Cleveland and Dallas–Ft. Worth approved the new taxes, so they were able directly to protect their own interests. But it is less clear if voters can sort through the complexities of other stadium deals to determine if they truly benefit from a new ball park.

One complication in casting a rational vote is that the direct beneficiaries of the stadium may not be clear. A stadium authority might be created that oversees the financing, construction, and operation of the facility. One private investor may operate the scoreboard and sell advertising on it, a second private party may secure the concession contract, while a third may run the parking lots. Those revenues may be split among the private firms, the team that people have paid to see, and the state. Complex agreements about the assumption of cost overruns and the determination of maintenance requirements may further confuse the voter.

This diffusion of businesses makes it more difficult for citizens to figure out whether each party is carrying a proper share of responsibility. No doubt the lawyers, owners, and accountants are generally satisfied, at least when the deal is signed, but the public lacks both the time and the expertise to oversee deals that are hopelessly baroque.

The benefits that the stadium provides are also rather subjective. As we have seen, the economic returns of stadiums are sharply debated, but there seems little doubt that benefits would accrue perhaps more easily from a private operation than a public one. When the economic arguments for a new ball park have been made, they are supplemented with the sentimental points about how important the team is to the community. And this is where the voter needs to pay very close attention.

The long and short of the booster's argument is that a city is not major league if it lacks one of these franchises. Such an assessment is inevitably personal, but it seems that any community that is insecure enough to believe such a proposition is necessarily not "major league." No doubt these teams add something to the culture of a city, but the contention that the town becomes a second-rate shantytown if it refuses to throw its money at a major league owner is false.

Each of the pending proposals for new ball parks needs to be examined on its own merits. Each plan will be unique in certain respects, and so will the circumstances in each city that considers a new facility. The common element in all cities at all times is that the major league franchises are enormously wealthy businesses, and compared with other public responsibilities, their importance is secondary. The money that stadiums now cost and the potential for a city to become hostage to an owner makes it imperative for citizens to have a compelling say in how their resources will be spent.

One way to analyze any stadium proposal is to compare it with three common models of economic development. The first is the familiar free market theory that attracts so much rhetorical support even while many of its advocates pursue every form of government aid possible. In the context of stadiums, a major league owner would have to acquire a site for a new ball park by purchasing land from the current owners.

Jack Kent Cooke did just that when he built the Forum in Inglewood, California, for the Los Angeles Lakers and Kings during the 1960s. Cooke bought the Inglewood Country Club next to the Hollywood Park Race Track and built the arena that has hosted Magic Johnson and Wayne Gretzky. But in most cases a stadium site will have multiple owners, all of whom can increase the value of their property simply by holding out and becoming the indispensable link in the project.

Even when Charlie Ebbets built the Dodgers' ball park in Brooklyn in 1910, he sent agents to Europe to find the owner of the last parcel of land that he needed. The gentleman turned out to be living in New Jersey, and, unaware of Ebbets's plans, he sold the lot to the Dodgers for $500. Keeping plans for a new stadium secret while acquiring the necessary land is not a serious possibility nowadays, so the free market model would mean that new private stadium construction without any governmental assistance is unlikely.

The economic model that has guided most modern stadium building is socialism. Marxism has collapsed all over the world, but it still holds an appeal to major league baseball owners. When government builds and maintains sports facilities, there are strong pressures to design the stadium or arena for as many purposes as possible. A sport with the eccentric geometry of baseball invariably suffers in such a setting.

The maintenance of a public stadium may be another problem. When budgets are strained, living with a little more filth at the ball park may be easier to accept than fewer police officers or health care workers. In New York City, bridges now require enormously expensive structural repairs because rust-preventing paint was not applied in a timely manner. Similar shortsighted economies risk turning stadiums into obsolete ruins long before their time.

The Detroit Tigers' efforts to replace their ball park show the strange attraction of the socialist stadium. The Tigers' owner, Tom Monaghan, is an almost legendary figure in the game. Talk about a Horatio Alger story—from a childhood in a Catholic orphanage, he became the phenomenally wealthy owner of Domino's Pizza before buying the Tigers. Monaghan has been tireless in promoting his understanding of Christian values in corporate settings, encouraging fellow business executives to maintain ethical values.

Monaghan is joined in the Tigers front office by Bo Schembechler, the former football coach at the University of Michigan. Both men are famous for teaching the values of self-reliance, hard work, and dedication to a goal, and both demonstrate how those qualities pay off.

Why then do the Tigers insist that the bankrupt city of Detroit build the team a new stadium?

The public-private partnership is the third model of economic development that can apply to stadiums, and it may become the most common. At a minimum, government assistance is likely to be needed for site acquisition and infrastructure. In principle, that should be the limit of government's involvement, as the major league franchise assumes the rest of the obligation. When the state becomes involved in financing and operating the facility, the same problems associated with Marxist stadiums can arise.

The variations on the public-private partnership are unlimited, but a strong bias should work in favor of simplicity. The deal needs to be accessible to citizens and taxpayers, who have their own pressing financial concerns that preclude their being authorities on the latest intricacies of municipal finance. At all times, citizens and their government representatives need to remember that sports franchises are entertainment businesses. They are not indispensable to the community. They provide us with fun and games, not food and water.

These businesses are immensely profitable. They are eminently capable of building some kind of stadium or making do with a current facility. The assumption that every new stadium has to outdo everything currently in use is as preposterous as thinking that every new sporting goods store in America has to be grander than Abercrombie & Fitch. Each team should calculate what every other business in its town must calculate: what is the best facility for me to operate given my resources and market?

Many healthy political battles will erupt over the stadiums that are going to be built in the next generation. No single example need be followed in every case, but the principle of the team carrying the burden of finance and maintenance is a good guide. With the magnificent improvements in stadium architecture, the Astroturf doughnuts may be relegated to professional football.

THE DIAMOND REVOLUTION

NOTES

1. Hearings Before the Antitrust Subcommittee of the Committee of the Judiciary, House of Representatives, *Organized Professional Team Sports*, 85th Cong, 1st sess., 2047.
2. Peter O'Malley, interview, O'Malley's office, August 19, 1991.
3. See Irving Kristol, *Two Cheers for Capitalism*. (New York: Basic Books, 1972).
4. "Inside the Shadowy Empire of Eli Jacobs," *Business Week*, November 18, 1991, pp. 116–20.
5. Fehr interview.
6. Janet Marie Smith, interview, Smith's office, August 2, 1990.
7. Baade, Robert, *Is There an Economic Rationale for Subsidizing Sports Stadiums?* (Chicago: The Heartland Institute, 1987), p. 18.
8. Quoted in Ralph Zolkos, "Cities Blast Stadium Study," *City and State* (April 1987): 3.
9. See Dennis Zimmerman, *The Private Use of Tax-Exempt Bonds: Controlling Public Subsidy of Private Activity* (Washington, D.C.: Urban Institute Press, 1991).
10. "An Overview of PFM's Sports Facilities and Convention Center Financing Practice," Public Financial Management, Inc., Philadelphia, PA, 19103.
11. Sam Katz, interview, Katz's office, October 1, 1990.

5

Expanding the Business—Cheapening the Game?

Peter Bavasi may know as much about expansion teams as anyone in baseball. He ran both the San Diego Padres and the Toronto Blue Jays during their formative years, and he tried to rouse the Cleveland Indians from senescence. When asked if the new National League franchises in Denver and Miami are worth the $95 million apiece that was paid, he replies that he would have recommended a counteroffer of $50 million.[1] As for the balance, he would have told the major leagues to perform a physiological impossibility with it. In Bavasi's view, no club in baseball is worth $95 million unless, like the Dodgers and Cardinals, it owns land.

Where did the $95 million figure come from? Since the San Diego Padres sold for $75 million in 1990 and the Seattle Mariners went for $68 million in 1989, the major league owners were emboldened to ask for the moon—specifically, a 1,350% increase in the price of admission since the last expansion round in 1977. In addition to the prevailing market price for a major league franchise, the prospect of heavy damages from collusion inspired the owners to look to expansion as a way to take the curse off their fines.

National publications have discussed Tom Werner's efforts to break even in San Diego and Jeff Smulyan's massive losses in Seattle. Would the buyers for new expansion teams be deterred by those struggles? Well, the biggest problem faced by the major league owners was how to say no to the four other expansion finalists whose money would *not* be pouring into the treasuries of the established clubs.

This last round of expansion confirmed many fans' worst suspicions about the greed that is rampant in baseball. The American and National leagues wrangled over the split of the expansion purse until Fay Vincent dictated a solution and chided the owners for their inability to settle the problem themselves. But if the owners are motivated by greed, then one question becomes very puzzling: if six ownership groups in six different cities were willing to pay $95 million apiece, why not admit all of them instead of turning down $380 million?

Some owners were concerned about the ability of each of the six finalists to actually come up with the $95 million, but cutting the admission fee to $50 million would have alleviated that problem and still brought the majors more than $100 million more than they made under the present arrangement. Whither greed?

Expansion of the major leagues pits two groups, each with strange allies, against each other. The major league owners have consistently resisted calls for increasing the number of teams, and they have been supported by purists who insist that the quality of the game deteriorates every time new teams are added.

The proponents of expansion include the Players Association, which maintains that the major league cartel artificially restricts the number of teams and jobs far below what a free market would produce. Joining with the union are boosters of major league baseball in many cities that have hosted minor league ball, members of Congress, and other politicians who want to secure a team for their constituents.

Despite the benefits that expansion brings—a shot of cash to each of the owners, new markets, and a placated Congress—keeping the major league markets under tight control has always been a dominant organizational goal of the major league owners. The game could have been organized very differently, with the numerous professional leagues across the country loosely affiliated.[2] Instead, the major league owners have consistently made conscious decisions that kept the American and National leagues at a higher level than their potential competitors.

The history of the relationship between the major and minor leagues is strong evidence that monopoly power is the paramount value of the major league owners. It is ironic that one of the architects of the majors' stifling control of the minors became one of the champions of expansion.

Branch Rickey earned his place in the Hall of Fame for a long career of innovative leadership, including his signing of Jackie Robinson, but nothing could have endeared him to the hearts of the major league owners more than one achievement: he saved the majors from any more Lefty Groves.

Grove exemplified one course of player development that briefly challenged the major league monopoly. The brilliant left-hander was discovered by Jack Dunn, owner of the Baltimore Orioles of the International League, pitching for Martinsburg of the Blue Ridge League in 1920. Dunn had discovered Babe Ruth in Baltimore but was forced to sell him to the Red Sox in 1914 when financial pressures from the Federal League nearly broke the Orioles. Dunn was thereafter determined never to part with a player for less than his market value.

Dunn purchased Grove's contract from Martinsburg for $3,500 to begin an investment that did not balance the loss of Ruth but came close. During five years with the Orioles, Grove's record was 109–6. Baltimore won the International League pennant every year, and every year major league clubs drooled at the prospect of having Grove in their uniform.

THE DIAMOND REVOLUTION

Under the prevailing agreement between the major leagues and the minors, International League players were not subject to a major league draft. If a major league club wanted Grove, it would have to pay a fair market price for him. By 1924, Connie Mack could stand it no longer, and he, of all people, paid Dunn $100,600 for Grove's contract, the largest amount paid for a player to that point.

Grove's rise to the big leagues was the way player development should proceed, according to Jack Dunn. In his view, minor league clubs were independent businesses located in smaller markets than the major league franchises. The minors were not subordinate to the majors in any respect, perhaps even in quality: Dunn's Orioles, considered to be one of the best teams in the history of minor league baseball, were almost certainly superior to some of the major league clubs in the 1920s.

Minor league clubs as independent businesses were free to sell or trade players to major league clubs at whatever price the market would bear. Because of their higher revenues, one would expect major league clubs to be able to pay higher salaries than the minors, thus attracting better players. But the gap between major league pay and the high minors was not the chasm that it is now, and some players actually preferred to play in places like California, which had compensations that a slight salary increase could not match.

Independence for the minors came with a price, one that was perilously high for many of the minor league operators. The price was that you were on your own when the winds of the economy blew cold. Dunn himself was chased out of Baltimore when the Federal League opened a franchise in town, and relatively few minor league owners were willing to take on the fight that Jack Dunn relished.

The alternative to independence was some kind of affiliation with a major league patron. The National Agreement of 1903 that brought peace to organized baseball established a hierarchy for the game, with the major leagues presiding over a tier of minor leagues. Formal ownership of the minor league clubs by the majors was ostensibly banned, but the majors were given the right to draft a limited number of players from associated minor league clubs in exchange for a modicum of money.

The arrangement indicated that the purpose of minor league baseball was muddled. The minors simultaneously represented professional baseball to the smaller communities of America at the same time they served as a training ground for the major leagues. Generations of Americans grew up cheering their local heroes in scintillating pennant races while they kept one ear cocked for the call that would pull an indispensable player from the team.

By 1920, strong pressures for independent minor leagues were being applied. First, the minors had taken a financial beating during World War I without any help from their nominal patrons. Only twenty minor leagues began the 1917 season, with twelve limping to the finish. Nine circuits tried to operate the following year, but only the International League made it through the season. Pleas to the majors for assistance were unavailing.

The American and National leagues were having problems of their own. The war, coming on the heels of the Federal League challenge, had been a terrible financial burden for the major league owners. Myopia more than malice is the probable reason they were unresponsive to the plight of the minors.

When the existing National Agreement expired in 1919, the high minors petitioned for a draft exemption and for higher draft compensation for the lower minors. The major leagues were unreceptive, and the organized leagues operated without formal ties for several years.

The majors' problems became critical with the revelation in 1920 of the Black Sox scandal. The future of organized baseball was in peril, and the major league owners accepted some significant reforms to preserve their business.

Among the changes was the introduction of the office of

commissioner of baseball. The first occupant, Judge Kenesaw Mountain Landis, was a strong believer in independent minor leagues. He also believed in a universal draft so that players could not be stuck on a team that would not give them a chance to develop their talents fully.

A new National Agreement was struck in 1921, shortly after Landis's election. Minor leagues were given the right to choose exemption from the draft if they too passed up drafting players from lower minor leagues.

In that climate, Jack Dunn demonstrated what an aggressive, talented executive could do when his Orioles won seven consecutive International League pennants from 1919 through 1925. Lefty Grove was only one of the players whom Dunn picked up, developed, and sold to a major league franchise for a sum far greater than the $5,000 draft compensation.

The model for player development that Dunn espoused was too expensive and too unpredictable for the major league owners. They preferred a way to bring players to their rosters that allowed them to keep their costs down and to retain control over their talent. Branch Rickey provided that mechanism through his refinement of the farm system. The National Agreement of 1921 allowed major league teams to own minor league teams, and Rickey used that opportunity to build the first comprehensive system for identifying, recruiting, and developing major league talent.

The benefits for his St. Louis Cardinals were apparent as the Gashouse Gang dominated the National League in the 1930s. The Yankees were one of the major league clubs that quickly applied Rickey's lessons, and the dynasty in New York was further secured through this device. When Rickey left the Cardinals for the Dodgers, Brooklyn soon had the basis for the Boys of Summer.

A carefully developed farm system had obvious benefits for the major league teams, but its impact on the minors was more dubious. In one of the worst instances, Rickey's Cardinals had agreements with both Springfield and Danville in the

Three-I League, thoroughly compromising the integrity of that circuit's pennant race.

Landis came down hard on Rickey for that breach, liberating seventy-four players from the Cardinals' farms to free agency. The rebuke was only a pause in the development of an empire that culminated in the ownership of thirty-two minor league clubs, working agreements with another eight, and a total of more than 600 players in the Cardinals system.

Such patronage enabled many minor league franchises to weather the Great Depression and World War II, but the lure of independence continued to appeal to some minor league officials, and it remained the moral choice of the commissioner. The campaign of the Pacific Coast League to become a third major league indicates that despite the success of the farm system, a strong desire for independence persisted in the minors.

The PCL's threat to pull out of organized baseball was the last salvo before the minors collapsed. In 1949, more than 40 million people saw games in fifty-nine minor leagues. By 1963, fewer than 10 million fans attended games in eighteen minor leagues.

The push for independent minors had been routed in an economic disaster that left long-established leagues distorted beyond recognition. The high minors were the most visibly affected. The American Association went out of existence from 1963 to 1968. The Pacific Coast League went through a bizarre contortion. In 1961, the Sacramento Solons became the Hawaii Islanders. Two years later, Vancouver pulled out of the league, but Denver, Dallas–Ft. Worth, and Oklahoma City were added. Indianapolis and Little Rock were acquired from the International League in 1964, making the PCL a twelve-team circuit. The league that had its roots in the 19th century, that had been one of the top associations in organized baseball, that had carved a distinct niche in the sport, and that had aspired to the pinnacle of the business had been reduced to a twelve-team caricature scattered across six time zones.

The goals of independent minor leagues were now a memory, but even the objective of player development was compromised by the chaos that threatened the minors. In 1962, the major leagues adopted the Player Development Plan, which made the minors outright wards of major league franchises. The new agreement eliminated the lowest strata of the minors by consolidating classes B through D into Rookie Leagues. Classes A through AAA were preserved, with each major league club owning a minor league affiliate in each classification.

The minors' collapse bottomed out with about ten million fans attending games in the eighteen to twenty leagues that still operated. The American Association came back in 1969, returning the PCL to eight teams, most of which were at least near to the Pacific Ocean.

In the 1970s, the majors began to rid themselves of the ownership of the minor league affiliates while continuing to pay their operating costs and retaining control of their rosters. The decision to sell the minor league franchises proved to have a dramatic effect on the relationship between the majors and minors.

Under local ownership, the hapless franchises of baseball began to prosper. Boosters hyped teams with Barnum-like enthusiasm. *Marketing* became the watchword of these clubs as they turned into one of the great investments of the 1980s. Some teams were purchased for a dollar, and they were later sold for tens of thousands. Triple A teams bought for a few hundred thousand were soon worth millions.

The key element of the prosperity was that the new owners faced negligible operating costs because the major league patron paid all the salaries. Facing little expense, whatever revenues could be gleaned from attendance or a broadcast contract were close to pure profit. And as the nation's affection for baseball returned, more people became interested in owning clubs for the fun of it.

Major league franchises were enormous investments reserved for the most wealthy, but thousandaires could seriously think about picking up a minor league club, and many did. With more potential owners chasing a fixed supply of teams, the value of individual franchises soared, and the local operators who took clubs off the hands of major league franchises found that they could resell the team for a sizable profit.

By the end of the 1980s, the majors had lost their sense of humor about the minors' good fortune. Some executives were taken aback that some of the minor league teams were actually turning an operating profit. It was one thing to clean up on the equity, quite another to clear annual profits while all the serious costs were picked up by the major league patron.

When the Player Development Contract expired in the winter of 1991, the major leagues were determined to redress the imbalance that they saw. They began by announcing that they would no longer subsidize the minor league teams. Independence was now a threat that the majors used to try to intimidate the minors into a more favorable arrangement.

Commissioner Fay Vincent announced that the majors were prepared to go a different route with player development, bypassing the minors entirely. Baseball academies would be established that would train the recruits in the intricacies of the game.

Interestingly, Vincent's threat was not far from the mind of Marvin Miller. Miller sees such camps as a means for the major league owners to cut their costs.[3] Because the business is a monopoly protected by law, he argues that teams could pool their training resources and instruct their recruits in common.

Rather than pursue the drastic and unlikely step of common training facilities, the majors announced that they would create new minor league franchises and simply transfer their financial assistance to the new clubs. An agreement was finally reached that preserves the primacy of the majors, limits minor league independence to a few franchises in the low minors, and keeps the principal goal of minor league baseball the development of players for the majors.

The cost of that development is likely to continue to rise. Financial burdens for equipment, coaches, trainers, and other expenses will undoubtedly grow. The pressure of those costs may lead some teams to bring players to the big leagues before they are quite ready. And as the salaries for veteran players rise further, owners may be inclined to replace them with rookies, even ones whose game may not quite be up to major league caliber.

An alternative to a long apprenticeship in the minors is college baseball, and the majors seem to be leaning more in that direction. In the first eight years of the major league draft, a majority of prospects were signed out of high school. The trend since 1973 has increasingly tilted to college players.

Players Signed in the June Draft[4]

YEAR	HIGH SCHOOL	COLLEGE	YEAR	HIGH SCHOOL	COLLEGE
1965	226	194	1978	172	330
1966	223	255	1979	158	423
1967	341	234	1980	157	439
1968	294	254	1981	113	521
1969	340	271	1982	139	481
1970	305	257	1983	125	493
1971	269	252	1984	117	506
1972	247	236	1985	119	537
1973	232	240	1986	142	506
1974	211	220	1987	170	629
1975	188	222	1988	190	701
1976	199	282	1989	207	623
1977	197	332			

The best college programs might be equivalent to Class A or even Double A minor league ball, so a major league fran-

112

chise can economize significantly by letting a college provide some of the basic training. Two problems with college baseball may need to be addressed in the future.

The first problem concerns race. Relying on college players may be one of the factors that is reducing the number of blacks who are playing the game. College has not been a barrier for blacks in basketball and football, but both those sports are far more visible on the collegiate level and thereby attractive to high school athletes. If college baseball becomes as glamorous as football and basketball, that may alleviate some of the slippage in black participation. But the College World Series remains, in the public eye, far behind major bowl games and the Final Four.

The technological problem with college baseball is the aluminum bat. Some speculate that pitchers do not learn how to pitch on the inside part of the plate because the pitch that might break a wooden bat on the handle could be looped safely in the outfield by a metal bat. Aluminum also lets the ball be hit farther and harder, distorting the ability of a prospect.

The major leagues might see the benefits of player development if they encourage baseball at every level short of the professional ranks. Perhaps a foundation could be established to help communities maintain suitable playgrounds with proper coaching. Similar support could help high school programs that are jeopardized by budget cuts. And some assistance to colleges might permit the retiring of the aluminum bat.

Despite the evidence of enthusiasm for baseball at the amateur and minor league levels, the record of expansion is that the major leagues add franchises as a reaction to outside pressure rather than as part of a strategic design to capitalize on the country's changing demographics and interests. The postwar period was an important time to think about the future of major league baseball and the adjustments that should be made to promote the game. Several compelling facts could have been considered during the late 1940s.

The first was that attractive markets lay outside the major league realm. California was certain to grow along with other western states. Cities in the Midwest such as Milwaukee, Minneapolis–St. Paul, and Kansas City were also appealing. Birthrates during the late 1940s anticipated the tremendous growth that would fuel the entire economy for decades.

Attendance records in Cleveland and Brooklyn in the late 1940s showed that baseball held possibilities for unprecedented prosperity. Baseball collectively had done well after previous wars, and the same could have been anticipated following the victory over Germany and Japan. The records of the Indians and the Dodgers after integration should have dispelled any lingering concerns about the effects of race on attendance.

Radio and television were a complication for the gate. Television was thought by many to be a passing fashion that would not find a secure place in the culture. The country was booming and eager to play, but what forms would the entertainment take, and how would baseball be affected? Policies that would take advantage of this revolution in broadcasting were desperately needed.

In 1950, without knowing all the details, no one should have thought that baseball would look the same in ten years. How could ten cities be expected to satisfy the demands for baseball? Expansion, realignment, and possibly the dissolution of some teams would have seemed inevitable in any other industry, but the major league owners responded in an ad hoc manner, with franchise moves rather than a comprehensive plan that would attempt to accommodate all organized baseball.

The opportunity to reorganize the business for modern times seems to have been taken as a threat to be resisted to the last possible moment. This defensive posture affected a number of business decisions, and it certainly shaped the path that expansion would take.

Expanding the Business—Cheapening the Game?

While the major leagues were preoccupied with World War II, the Pacific Coast League called for a bold change in organized baseball. The PCL president, Clarence "Pants" Rowland, proposed at the winter meetings of 1945 that the Coast League be elevated to a third major league.

At the time, the league consisted of the Seattle Rainiers, the Portland Beavers, the Sacramento Solons, the Oakland Oaks, the San Francisco Seals, the Los Angeles Angels, the Hollywood Stars, and the San Diego Padres. Some franchises had strong financial bases, while others were rather marginal—a point that could also be made about the American and National leagues.

As a league, the PCL was distinct in organized baseball. It sometimes had taken advantage of the mild climate by extending its seasons to 200 games. Baseball in the West was often played from Easter to Thanksgiving. Smead Jolley, Buzz Arlett, Ike Boone, and Ox Eckhardt were some of the players who enjoyed distinguished careers in the Coast League, and the Los Angeles Angels of 1934 were one of the greatest minor league teams ever.

Whether the PCL in the mid-1940s was as good as the National and American leagues is doubtful. Many of the great Coast League stars never amounted to much in their brief major league careers. Jigger Statz, for example, compiled more than 3,300 hits during his years in the Coast League, but his major league numbers were unremarkable. Frank Shellenback won 295 games on the coast but only ten in two big-league seasons.

On the face of it, perhaps major league talent was simply not plentiful enough to reach eight more teams, but Coast League officials had a different explanation. They saw their best players drafted by the American and National League teams with but a pittance to compensate the franchise that had developed the player. The critical step that PCL officials sought after World War II was an exemption from the major league draft. Given the chance to develop and keep their best players, they were convinced that they could reach parity with the established big-league clubs.

One aspect of the PCL proposal that fell on deaf ears was that they were offering not only individual ball clubs for major league consideration but an entire league. Organized baseball had been played in California as long as it had been played in New York, and the Coast League was offering to bring that heritage to the major leagues.

Entrepreneurs who had developed their teams over many years, club names, uniform designs and ball parks that had been familiar for decades, traditional and newly created rivalries, and a local pride in the sporting history—all these factors were potentially powerful marketing forces to promote a third major league.

The appeal of that heritage was lost on the American and National leagues, which could only see the potential of Los Angeles and San Francisco without any appreciation for the value of the other communities of the Coast League. But when the majors finally came to the west, they gradually moved into all those markets except Sacramento and Portland, and they also acquired the names Angels and Padres.

A potential advantage of upgrading minor league teams for expansion is that they already have organizations in place. After Denver and Miami pay their separate $95 million bills, they face an estimated $25 million to $35 million to build front office staffs, and scouting and player development operations that minor league teams already have at least in a rudimentary form.

The proposal to expand the major leagues by a gradual upgrading of the minor leagues was rejected by the American and National leagues. By 1947, other minor leagues had lost patience with the Coast League's claims of superiority, and their support for the proposal became more tepid. In that year, Commissioner Chandler suggested major league expansion to California by adding four teams, two for each league in Los Angeles and San Francisco. That proposal received the unanimous support of the National League, but two dissenting votes in the American League doomed the idea.

The 1950s was a crucial period for expansion. The PCL request had become a demand accompanied by a threat to withdraw from organized baseball. In 1951, the major leagues squelched the bid through Commissioner Ford Frick. Frick raised the Coast League to an Open Classification or Four A status, putting the PCL between the other Triple A leagues and the majors. He then established the criteria that any Four A league would have to meet to be elevated to the majors: a total population of 15 million in the league's cities; each stadium with a capacity of at least 25,000; and total annual attendance of 3.5 million for three consecutive years.

The first two standards were easily met by the Coast League, but the final test had become insuperable. Television was beginning to erode minor league attendance as Milton Berle, Sid Caeser, and other stars kept fans in their living rooms. The golden age of minor league baseball had passed. By the 1960s, the minors would need substantial help from the majors simply to survive in a truncated and distorted form. The opportunity to expand the major leagues by upgrading the minors had died aborning.

Television had not only devastated the minors, but it had not yet done the major league teams much good. The high attendance figures of the late 1940s gradually dwindled over the next decade. Some teams, like the Dodgers, were making significant money by televising their games, but few clubs had a clear idea of what television meant and how it should be used.

Without a comprehensive plan to meet the postwar challenges, baseball had lurched through the tumultuous 1950s by moving five of its major league clubs into the top markets of a minor league system that was already reeling. Major league baseball added five new cities to its roster without putting a single new team in the National and American leagues.

THE DIAMOND REVOLUTION

The ambition of the Pacific Coast League should not be dismissed as impossible or necessarily damaging to baseball. If baseball had expanded by adding the PCL and at least some of the teams in the American Association and the International League, the structure of major league baseball would have been radically different from what we know, but perhaps the game would have been even more engaging.

In basketball, the worst team in the National Basketball Association would run the winner of the Final Four right off the court. Yet college basketball is a more popular sport than the professional version. College hoops saturate television compared with the NBA, yet the ratings and income show no sign of fans becoming bored with the "lesser" product.

By way of comparison, college basketball is a more exciting game than the NBA for many fans. It relies on rivalries and tradition, depending on the disparities of talent to set the stage for historic upsets, and it puts its arenas to effective use in staging this drama. The NCAA has shown that selling entertainment does not depend on having the best quality product. If the game is exciting and competitive, fans will be captivated.

Comparing NCAA basketball or football and minor league baseball is a far from perfect fit. The compensation to the athletes is one critical difference (one hopes). The point is that the assets that colleges use to market their sports could be used by baseball, but they have not always been.

Major league baseball has marketed itself on the proposition that it has the best players, and there is no argument there. But that is only one model for a successful sports enterprise. College sports rely on extending access to a sport to small communities that cannot match numbers with New York or Los Angeles. But when the small schools upset Notre Dame or Southern Cal, legends are born that can fuel support for a generation.

Without question, the PCL model for expansion would have significantly changed organized baseball and especially

118

the major leagues. But that change would not inevitably have lowered the majors to a level of unappealing mediocrity.

Having rejected the Pacific Coast League's plan and having no plan of their own, the major leagues finally expanded when they were threatened by Branch Rickey. The Continental League that Rickey assembled on paper in 1959 included sports impresarios like Joan Payson Whitney, Jack Kent Cooke, and Lamar Hunt. The eight-team league intended to put teams in Atlanta, Buffalo, Dallas–Ft. Worth, Denver, Houston, Minneapolis–St. Paul, New York, and Toronto.

Without playing a game, Rickey already anticipated expansion for the league to the cities of Honolulu, Montreal, New Orleans, San Diego, and Seattle. The plan was an obvious attempt to boldly go where the major leagues had been too timid to go. And while the scope of the Continental League seemed quixotic at the time, the major leagues eventually located in ten of the thirteen cities.

Recognizing that the bullying that had worked with the Coast League might not be effective against Rickey, the majors added their first new teams since Teddy Roosevelt was in the White House, and of those first four teams, only Houston was located in a previously untested market. The Angels joined the Dodgers in Los Angeles, and the Mets and the Senators moved into the recently vacated markets of New York and Washington, D.C.

The second major league expansion in 1969 added another four teams. Two of them, the Seattle Pilots and the San Diego Padres, lent quiet support to the legitimacy of the PCL's earlier aspirations. The Kansas City Royals were created to quell a political furor when the Athletics moved to the gold coast of California, and the Montreal Expos took the major leagues to Canada for the first time.

The third expansion added two clubs to the American League in 1977. The Toronto Blue Jays provided Labatt's with the same forum for selling beer that August Busch had enjoyed with the Cardinals, and the Seattle Mariners obvi-

119

ated the antitrust suit that the city had threatened since the Pilots flew to Milwaukee.

Of those ten new teams, five—the Astros, Blue Jays, Expos, Padres, and Pilots—were placed in untested markets, while the Angels and Mets went to certain prosperity in existing major league markets and the Mariners, Royals, and Senators covered the majors' exposed political flanks in abandoned cities.

The addition of teams to the American and National leagues raises the most fundamental question about the business of baseball: what is the nature of the product that is being sold? Should the majors be limited to only the very best players, or should a wider net bring major league ball to more communities? Few would challenge the claim that the major leagues offer the best baseball played anywhere in the world, but many people believe that the major league game is not what it used to be.

This question is critical for baseball's future. If the quality of the game is deteriorating, how long will fans continue to pay to see it? Baseball has done an impressive job of keeping ticket prices within reach of middle-class and working-class fans, but the hot dogs, beer, and peanuts that are an integral part of going to the ball park have begun to rival the price of dinner in a decent restaurant.

Consider the mythical family outing at which the game is marketed by one generation to another. If the family has four members who do not sit in the bleachers, do not bring their own food, and do park their car in a lot adjacent to the stadium, the outing can easily cost seventy dollars.

Whether they get their money's worth is almost entirely subjective, but a great many fans would gladly pay that amount or more to see future Hall of Famers at the peak of their career. The problem develops if the fan sees shabby or indifferent play: a batter walks on four pitches, the next hitter has a .250 average, but he swings at the first pitch; a rundown play takes so many throws to complete that it looks like a Rorschach test in the scorecard; worn spots appear in the outfield grass because every hitter is positioned the same way.

Nostalgia keeps whispering that pitchers were never walked with the bases loaded in the old days, that every batter could stroke a ground ball to the right side of the infield with a runner on second and nobody out, that every outfielder hit the cutoff man, and that every cutoff man was in the right position.

If the fans listen to the nostalgic voices, they may decide that major league baseball is not worth seventy bucks even if an owner thinks it is worth $95 million. If enough families stop coming to the park, then the franchise will in fact not be worth $95 million, and that will be the end of this most lucrative age.

One certain way to preserve the quality of major league baseball is to restrict the number of teams and players to only the very best. Such a limitation counters the pressure for major league baseball to expand to cities that want their own ball clubs. Whenever new teams have been added, cries go up that the quality of the game is going to suffer, and, by implication, baseball could become less attractive as a result of inferior play.

Expansion raises this question for baseball: is the product watered down by adding teams to the major leagues? Sometimes critics focus on the additional players that expansion brings to the big leagues and conclude that they represent athletes who would have been left in the minors in a better day.

That argument assumes that major league players are special gifts of nature who are acutely small in number. True enough, but the number of major leaguers likely bears some relationship to the number of the rest of us. Why think that there are x number of major leaguers regardless of the size of the population? To think that expansion inevitably deteriorates the quality of baseball requires one to believe that as the country has grown, baseball's labor pool has remained static. The alternative view, that the potential major leaguers are a constant proportion of the population, means that their numbers will grow as the community increases. If again we use the standard that baseball is played by men between the ages of twenty and forty, we can see a remarkable development over the history of the major league game.

Percentage of Population in the Major Leagues

CENSUS	MALES AGES 20–39[5]	MAJOR LEAGUERS	RATIO
1900	11,068,157*	400	1:27,670
1910	14,184,350	400	1:35,460
1920	15,174,484	400	1:37,936
1930	17,413,164	400	1:43,533
1940	18,833,339	400	1:47,083
1950	22,855,322**	400	1:57,138
1960	22,531,151***	500	1:45,062
1970	25,547,049	650	1:39,303
1980	35,906,643	650	1:55,241
1990†	41,577,000	700	1:59,396

* White males only, 1900–40.
** All races, 1950–present.
*** The decline in the pool from 1950 to 1960 is likely a result of marriages deferred by the Great Depression and World War II.
† Estimate.
NOTE: The ratio for the 1960s is calculated by taking the census of 1960 as a pool for the sixteen original major league teams plus the four expansion teams of 1961 and 1962. The 1970s ratio compares the population figures with the first twenty major league clubs plus the four teams added in 1969 and the two that joined in 1977.

Prior to 1990 and the Miami-Denver expansion, the average ratio of major league player to the available American labor pool was 1 in 43,158. The thrilling National League pennant race of 1908 is remembered as not only excruciatingly close but also reflective of the excellent baseball at that time—Christy Mathewson and the Giants, Mordecai Brown and the Cubs, Honus Wagner and the Pirates. Each of those brilliant players was culled from a far smaller pool than what has normally been available to baseball.

Ty Cobb, Napoleon Lajoie, Joe Jackson, and Babe Ruth all got to the big leagues from a smaller population base than what would later be the case. The Yankees of Joe McCarthy and the Gashouse Gang in St. Louis were drawn from the statistically average pool that the game has enjoyed. The 1940s are an anomaly because of the effects of World War II, but thereafter the demographics strongly tilt in the direction of expansion.

The highest the ratio ever had been was the decade of the 1950s, the period many of us look back on with such fondness. After four teams were added in the early 1960s, that high mark dropped, but major league players were still a smaller part of the population than they had been in the 1930s.

The ratio dipped below the level of the 1930s when a total of six clubs were added in 1969 and 1977, but that still meant that major leaguers were a smaller elite of the overall pool than their predecessors had been up through the 1927 Yankees.

By 1980, the baby boomers were old enough to play, and the ratio jumped back nearly to its peak of the 1950s. Another decade of growth in the pertinent group of males means that even after Miami and Denver have been added to the National League, the ratio of major leaguer to the labor pool will be higher than ever before. To the familiar complaint that the game is not what it used to be, the evidence suggests that plenty of quality players should be available for major league rosters.

Another way of crunching these numbers is to consider this: if the quality of major league baseball in its first decade of the modern era was satisfactory, then how many clubs could be competing today at that level? By dividing the sixteen major league teams into the labor pool of 1900, we determine that each club represents 691,760 of the white male population ages 20–39. As the potential pool expanded through integration and population growth, it boomed far beyond the pace of expansion.

By the 1950s, thirty-two major league clubs could have been operating at the ratio of one team for roughly 700,000 males ages 20–39. In the 1990s, *sixty* teams could be in the major leagues without diluting the quality that prevailed in a decade that included Wee Willie Keeler, Jack Chesbro, Sam Crawford, Cy Young, Rube Waddell, and Eddie Plank as well as Cobb, Lajoie, Mathewson and Wagner, not to mention Tinker to Evers to Chance.

This analysis does not mean that sixty teams *should* now be in the major leagues. Many factors dictate the success of a major league franchise, including the ability to find and develop the talent that is available: the greatest second baseman in history may have remained undiscovered in a dry cleaner in Dubuque.

The analysis does help to dispel the hoary claim that expansion necessarily damages the quality of the game by diluting the legitimate major league players with mediocre wannabes. Finding and developing the men with the gifts to play major league baseball has always been one of the supreme challenges of any front office. But to the question of whether the talent is out there, the answer seems eminently clear: If 400 young men were good enough to play major league baseball in 1900, it is not statistically unreasonable to conclude that 1,500 are equally qualified now.

One important complication with these numbers is the attraction of basketball and football for athletes who want to make a career in sports. Bo Jackson, Dave Winfield, Orel Hershiser, and Deion Sanders are among the talented young men who either do or could make a living at any of several professional sports. But the competitive pull of the other major sports is inherently limited.

While every professional athlete is physically exceptional, major league baseball players come in sizes that more nearly resemble normal people. Very few baseball players could play power forward or center in the NBA, and probably none could be an interior lineman in the NFL. No doubt the growth of those other sports has claimed some potential major league players, but the nature of the other games limits baseball-sized players to a few select positions.

Al Rosen, general manager of the San Francisco Giants, believes that the NBA and the NFL have taken a number of players who could have been stars in the major leagues.[6] The potential baseball player would not likely be playing the low post or leading a power sweep, but Rosen thinks that a significant number of point guards and wide receivers would be on the diamond if the NBA and the NFL did not offer an alternative.

He adds that tennis and golf have also attracted men who might have become baseball players. Bill Tilden and Bobby Jones were stars from those sports when Babe Ruth played, but the purses available in the country club sports now make them competitive with the growth of baseball.

In a rare agreement of labor and management, Donald Fehr believes also that the other professional sports may significantly divert talent from baseball.[7] As Fehr sees it, basketball and football provide an opportunity to get a college education, whereas baseball sidetracks some players to the minor leagues. The college game also focuses primarily on winning and not on player development, the primary interest of the major leagues.

To Fehr's point, it seems at least as plausible that baseball would appeal to some athletes who would rather begin a professional career right after high school rather than deferring a salary for four years. Baseball gives an athlete who is academically unqualified a respectable alternative to the disreputable charades that some colleges have used to secure football and basketball players.

Rosen's opinion about the draw of other sports must be respected because he has had such an extensive and successful career finding talent for major league clubs. But his argument about the increased appeal of other sports could be another factor that actually mitigates the effects of expansion.

The growing appeal of other professional sports reflects that the status of sports has grown significantly in this country, making a career as a professional athlete an estimable pursuit in the minds of most people. Earlier in the century, a baseball player might have had the same cachet as a professional wrestler—not something that parents would want to see their college graduate pursue.

A professional athlete now has more choices than a career in baseball, but the initial decision to become a professional athlete is socially much more acceptable than it was when Christy Mathewson defied convention or when Lou Gehrig disappointed his mother. The first-class travel and accommodations that players now insist upon are rather taken for granted by the public, a sign that athletes are an accepted part of the rich and famous.

The quality of major league baseball is one consideration of expansion. Another is competitiveness. Peter Bavasi makes the point that the quality of the expansion teams could be established from the beginning by a more realistic draft of existing major league players.[8] By sticking the new clubs with the marginal players, the owners guarantee a couple of soft touches for the home team for at least a few years. Leagues are then distorted, with the established clubs operating at an obviously higher level than the newcomers.

The major leagues' policy on expansion drafts reflects the same priority that has made expansion so difficult: established teams passionately hate losing players that they have developed. An expansion draft has some of the features of free agency except that the bereft club does not get even a draft pick in return. Consequently, the expansion drafts have been arranged so that at most, a team might lose three players from its forty-man roster.

Expanding the Business—Cheapening the Game?

The justification for charging a fee to the clubs who are entering the majors is largely because they will be stocked with players who were developed by other organizations. Defraying those expenses is only a fair compensation. If the existing rosters were opened beyond the bottom two-fifths to the nucleus of the club, then figuring a fair return would be perhaps hopelessly complicated. As things stand, the expansion clubs pay a princely sum to climb aboard, then face years of financial losses along with a usually dreadful record on the field.

The record of previous expansion clubs shows their varying successes in the struggle first for respectability, then glory:

Expansion Club Finishes

TEAM	YEAR OF ORIGIN	FIRST YEAR OUT OF THE CELLAR	REACHES .500	SOME KIND OF CHAMPIONSHIP
Angels	1961	1961	1962	1979
Rangers	1961	1964*	1969	——
Mets	1962	1966	1969	1969
Astros	1962	1962	1969	1980
Expos	1969	1971	1979	1981**
Padres	1969	1975	1978	1984
Royals	1969	1969	1971	1976
Brewers	1969	1970	1978	1981***
Blue Jays	1977	1983†	1983	1985
Mariners	1977	1977	1991	——

*As did the expansion Washington Senators, the club finished its first year tied for seventh place with the Athletics.

**The Expos made the playoffs during the strike season by winning the divisional playoff in the NL East.

***The Brewers failed to make the playoffs during the 1981 season, but they did have the best overall record in the AL East. They won their first division title in 1982.

†The Blue Jays tied for sixth place in 1982.

One pattern suggests that expansion teams are poor until further expansion raises them to mediocrity. Three of the first four expansion teams did not reach .500 until four more teams were added in 1969. The Brewers hit that mark in 1978, two years after the Blue Jays and the Mariners joined the American League. But the Padres and the Expos, the National League's members of the class of 1969, took about the same time to play .500 ball without the benefit of further expansion in that league.

Reviewing the clubs individually, the Angels became a decent club very quickly, but they still have not managed a league pennant. The Rangers were not long the worst team in the American League, but they remain one of the few clubs that has not captured even a division title.

The Mets were perhaps the worst team in the history of baseball for their first few years, but no other expansion team has won a championship so quickly nor so dramatically. The Astros have labored in a pattern much like the Rangers—something about major league baseball in Texas.

The Expos took eleven years to get to .500, but a couple of years after that they were within a few outs of going to the World Series. The Padres have had some tough years in San Diego, but they are one of four expansion teams to have played in the Series.

The Brewers have also won a league pennant, and they have enjoyed some of the game's best players, including Robin Yount, Paul Molitor, and Teddy Higuera. The Blue Jays have quickly become one of the best organizations in baseball, but the Mariners needed fifteen seasons even to hit the .500 mark.

The ten expansion teams represent also a variety of different business strategies, beginning with the different entry fees charged to the newcomers. The Angels entered the American League after paying $2.1 million. They have remained from their beginnings in the hands of Gene Autry, who moved the club to Orange County in 1965 to get some breathing room from Walter O'Malley and the Dodgers. The team has drawn well in its stadium beside Disneyland, and Autry has run the club as a hobby, freely spending in pursuit of a pennant.

Two old guard owners: Connie Mack (left) of the Philadelphia Athletics and Clark Griffith of the Washington Senators. (*Photo courtesy International News Photos*)

Walter O'Malley, owner of the Brooklyn Dodgers. (*Photo courtesy National Baseball Library, Cooperstown, New York*)

A first in the history of the All-Star game: the first black players ever selected stand in Ebbets Field on July 12, 1949. Left to right: Roy Campanella, Larry Doby, Don Newcombe, and Jackie Robinson. (*Photo courtesy Acme*)

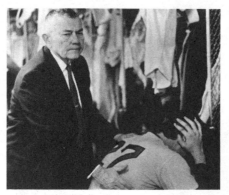

Boston Red Sox owner Tom Yawkey comforts Carlton Fisk after the Sox lost the 1972 American League pennant race to Detroit. (*Photo courtesy Frank O'Brien/ Boston Globe*)

Bill Veeck, Jr., one of baseball's maverick owners.

Ford Frick (right) comes to the rescue of new baseball commissioner
William Eckert during a storm of questions from reporters immediately
after Frick announced his retirement. (*Photo courtesy UPI*)

Rivals in the 1970s: Commissioner Bowie Kuhn (left) and Marvin Miller,
executive director of the players' association. (*Photos courtesy UPI*)

Atlanta Braves' owner Ted Turner, today's maverick. (*Photo courtesy National Baseball Library, Cooperstown, New York*)

One of the shrines of baseball: Boston's Fenway Park. (*Photo courtesy National Baseball Library, Cooperstown, New York*)

Brooklyn's Ebbets Field (above) vs. Dodger Stadium in Los Angeles.

Sportsman's Park (above) vs. Busch Stadium in St. Louis, the old and new homes of the Cardinals. (*Photos courtesy National Baseball Library, Cooperstown, New York*)

Shibe Park (above) vs. Veterans Stadium in Philadelphia, the old-style park and the modern donut design. (*Shibe Park photo courtesy National Baseball Library, Cooperstown, New York*)

Yankee Stadium from right field, before and after the renovation that improved sight lines by removing obstructions. (*Top photo courtesy Associated Press*)

Expanding the Business—Cheapening the Game?

The Texas Rangers were born in futility as the new Washington Senators for the same delivery fee of $2.1 million. If the Griffith family could not make a go of Washington D.C., why would an expansion team be expected to prosper in the same market and stadium? The experiment was a bust, and the new club moved to the Dallas area in 1969. It now seems secure with a terrific team in the AL West and plans for a new stadium.

The Mets joined the National League for $1.8 million, the lowest fee of the new entrants. They have prospered when the club has been either great or at least amazing. The one tough period for the franchise occurred in the late 1970s and early 1980s, when they were both dreadful and lackluster. They have confirmed the unsurprising proposition that New York is a great National League market.

The Astros have not fared so well in Houston. The club began as the Colt .45s for a $1.85 million entry fee. The franchise shed the cowboy motif for the space age when the Astrodome opened. In thirty years, they have not sustained a great team to build a solid foundation of support, and talk of a move to another city has recurred.

The second round of expansion in 1969 produced a similarly mixed record, as both the National and American leagues added two teams in the same year. The Kansas City Royals were forced into existence by Senator Stuart Symington of Missouri, who threatened the major leagues when the Athletics left for Oakland. The Royals were a bargain at $1.8 million, the same entry price as the Mets. The Royals have been a great success, quickly becoming one of the top clubs in the American League.

The Seattle Pilots came into the American League with the Royals, but for a steeper price. The Pilots paid $5.55 million to struggle through one year in the state of Washington. As the Milwaukee Brewers, the franchise is inevitably mentioned when the subject of small markets is discussed. Owner Bud Selig has articulately championed the point that the larger clubs must make more equitable financial arrangements with teams in smaller cities. But Selig has done well enough to plan to build the first privately financed stadium in baseball since 1962.

The San Diego Padres and the Montreal Expos entered the National League at the same time as the Royals and Pilots began, but the senior league nicked the newcomers for $12.5 million apiece. The Padres began under the ownership of the Smith brothers, who held the old Coast League franchise. The team nearly left California until Ray Kroc brought his hamburger wizardry to the rescue. Peter Bavasi fondly remembers Kroc's insistence that the Padres be run without reliance on the McDonald's treasury. Bavasi was told to pay the players out of his own pocket if he could not keep the team within its budget.

The Expos also started with the stiff $12.5 million bill. They put a very fine team together in the early 1980s, but when those players left there was little to sustain the fans' interest. The team plays in one of the worst stadiums in the game—it even managed a rainout in 1991 despite having a dome—and it is one of the franchises mentioned whenever relocation is discussed.

The third expansion in 1977 added two clubs to the American League, and they have gone in opposite directions. The Toronto Blue Jays are owned by the Labatt's Brewery, and it has built championship teams and drawn record crowds in Skydome. Despite the cost to the Expos to join the majors, the Blue Jays were billed a mere $7 million to enter the American League. They enjoy a reputation as one of the leading teams and businesses in baseball, and with that the expectations for a World Series championship are building.

The Mariners were an even greater bargain, joining the American League with the Blue Jays for but $6.25 million. Under former owner George Argyros, the Mariners let their best players leave and failed to market the club to their potential fans. Like Astros owner John McMullen, Argyros refused to pay the salaries that are necessary to hold or attract talent. While keeping his operating costs to a minimum, Argyros was able to sell the Mariners to Jeff Smulyan for $68 million, a sum that appears to be far too high for the value of the club.

The impediments to success that any expansion team can expect seem to take from five to ten years to overcome. The early histories of the Angels and the Royals are probably being astutely reviewed in Denver and Miami these days; but if either club wins as many games as it loses before the millennium, that should be a cause for celebration.

The impact of the Marlins and the Rockies on the rest of the game will be heartily discussed until the lads actually take the field, and the arguments will probably grow after that. The worst fears—that the most revered seasonal records will drop in a heap—are very unlikely. Roger Maris's sixty-one home runs after the first expansion are ever on the pessimists' mind, but the next year, Willie Mays led the National League with forty-nine homers, inspiring neither hysteria nor asterisks.

The leading statistics for 1969 are impressive but not shockingly different from other years. In fact, Bob Gibson's memorable ERA of 1.12 was posted in the 1968 season. The following year, Juan Marichal led the league with a mark of 2.10. Similarly, Denny McLain won his thirty-one games in 1968, and he led the American League in the year of expansion with twenty-four victories.

In 1977, George Foster became the first National Leaguer to hit at least fifty home runs since Willie Mays in 1965 (both hit fifty-two), but the expansion that year was in the American League, where Jim Rice led with thirty-nine homers.

The impact of expansion on familiar individual titles shows the following:

THE DIAMOND REVOLUTION

Impact of Expansion on Individual Titles

AMERICAN LEAGUE

TITLE	1960		1961 (EXPANSION YEAR)	
Home Runs	Mickey Mantle	40	Roger Maris	61
Batting	Pete Runnels	.320	Norm Cash	.361
RBIs	Roger Maris	112	Roger Maris	142
Wins	Chuck Estrada & Jim Perry	18	Whitey Ford	25
ERA	Frank Baumann	2.68	Dick Donovan	2.40

NATIONAL LEAGUE

TITLE	1961		1962 (EXPANSION YEAR)	
Home Runs	Orlando Cepeda	46	Willie Mays	49
Batting	Roberto Clemente	.351	Tommy Davis	.346
RBIs	Orlando Cepeda	142	Tommy Davis	153
Wins	Warren Spahn & Joey Jay	21	Don Drysdale	25
ERA	Warren Spahn	3.01	Sandy Koufax	2.54

AMERICAN LEAGUE

TITLE	1968		1969 (EXPANSION YEAR)	
Home Runs	Frank Howard	44	Harmon Killebrew	49
Batting	Carl Yastrzemski	.301	Rod Carew	.332
RBIs	Ken Harrelson	109	Harmon Killebrew	140
Wins	Denny McLain	31	Denny McLain	24
ERA	Luis Tiant	1.60	Dick Bosman	2.19

NATIONAL LEAGUE

TITLE	1968		1969 (EXPANSION YEAR)	
Home Runs	Willie McCovey	36	Willie McCovey	45
Batting	Pete Rose	.335	Pete Rose	.348
RBIs	Willie McCovey	105	Willie McCovey	126
Wins	Juan Marichal	26	Tom Seaver	25
ERA	Bob Gibson	1.12	Juan Marichal	2.10

AMERICAN LEAGUE

TITLE	1976		1977 (EXPANSION YEAR)	
Home Runs	Graig Nettles	32	Jim Rice	39
Batting	George Brett	.333	Rod Carew	.388
RBIs	Lee May	109	Larry Hisle	119
Wins	Jim Palmer	22	Jim Palmer, Dennis Leonard & Dave Goltz	20
ERA	Mark Fidrych	2.34	Frank Tanana	2.54

Expanding the Business—Cheapening the Game?

More likely than a seventy-home-run season, a .400 batting average, or thirty wins will be some young stars who are currently trapped in the minors or on a major league bench finally getting a chance to play. The eternal complaint of the prospect who fails to fulfill his potential is that he needs to play regularly against major league competition. Dozens of young men will get that opportunity, and some of them will be proved right.

If the expansion teams happen to do well on the field with young teams and presumably low payrolls, some baseball executives will growl at their high-priced talent and their struggles with injuries and equally talented opposition. Expansion is likely to have far more of an impact on the business of baseball than on the game itself.

The next round of expansion will occur when congressional pressure builds again or when the owners and the Players Association have framed a true partnership that lets the union apply some leverage internally. Nothing suggests that the owners will step back and examine the current state of their business to determine a sensible strategy for adding teams over the next ten to twenty years.

Further expansion will likely break the current system of scheduling and league alignments. Calls for interleague play will rise again, as will the resistance from those committed to the separate traditions of each league.

The major question will concern the quality of the game. As the cries go forth that the game is being diluted and reduced to an imitation of what we remember, advocates of expansion can reasonably claim that there is no reason why the quality of the game should be diminished.

The talented young men most likely are available. The trick is to find them, convince them that baseball is a worthwhile pursuit, and develop their skills. To achieve these goals, the majors should consider their relationships with the minor leagues, colleges, and youth baseball. Investments that bolster the stability and encourage growth at each of those levels will undoubtedly redound to the benefit of the majors.

NOTES

1. Bavasi interview.
2. See Neil Sullivan, *The Minors: The Struggles and the Triumph of Baseball's Poor Relation* (New York: St. Martin's Press, 1990).
3. Miller interview.
4. Baseball America, *The Baseball Draft: The First 25 Years* (Durham: American Sports Publishing, 1990), p. 6.
5. U.S. Bureau of the Census, *Historical Statistics of the United States Colonial Times to 1970* (Washington, DC: Government Printing Office, 1975), pp. 15–16.
6. Al Rosen, interview, Rosen's office, August 23, 1990.
7. Fehr interview.
8. Bavasi interview.

6

Broadcasting—A Network
in Every Home

Money from the pictures, descriptions, and accounts of the game has given baseball a Midas touch. Free agency and salary arbitration would not have driven salaries so high without a corresponding boom in teams' revenues. The source of the players' salaries is the television and radio money, the financial backbone of baseball.

Since the 1950s, ticket prices have risen below the rate of inflation while the growth of revenues from broadcasting (over-the-air transmissions of radio or television signals) and cable (transmissions through wire) has soared. The principals of major league baseball have become rich in the sport beyond their wildest imaginations, but, especially for the owners, the distribution of that purse has become an extremely contentious issue.

The current annual broadcast and cable yield includes about $250 million from CBS for each of its four years of the blockbusting $1.1 billion network contract, $100 million annually from ESPN in a concurrent four-year agreement, $12.5 million from CBS radio, and a balance of more than $150 million in local broadcast contracts. Money from the national contracts is divided equally among the twenty-six major league teams, but revenues from the local deals flow only to the

135

individual club that made the contract—a source of some distress for many teams. Even more disturbing are the staggering losses that CBS and ESPN have so far sustained in this deal. The next contract will likely mean lower revenues for baseball.

Figures compiled by *Sports Illustrated* show how important broadcast and cable money has become for baseball. Using 1990 dollars, television and radio put $17 million into the treasuries of the major leagues during the 1950 season, and forty years later, those media generated $625 million. More significant, in 1950, money from attendance was $122 million, about seven times greater than income from radio and television that year; but in 1990, attendance produced $503 million, more than $120 million *less* than the take from radio and television.

The primary place of broadcasting in the revenue stream is a big change from the 1950s (see table, page 137). Revenue figures from the 1956 season show a far less significant role for broadcasting for most of the sixteen major league teams.

The figures show how tight the spread of revenue was among the sixteen major league clubs. The Yankees, of course, made the most money—slightly more than $5 million, but the Indians managed an even larger broadcast deal. At the other end of the revenue scale, the Senators took in just $1,412,271; but the gross income of every other American League team fell between $2 million and $3 million.

In the National League, the Dodgers and the Braves grossed $3.8 million and $3.6 million, respectively. The Cubs lagged with $1.6 million, but every other team in the circuit took in between $2 million and $2.5 million. Half the teams in the league took in more money from road receipts than from their broadcast agreements. A gentlemen's club could operate with revenue spreads like that. The competition of a real market in transmitting the games was not only unseemly—it was unnecessary.

Broadcasting—A Network in Every Home

Income for the 1956 Season[1]

NATIONAL LEAGUE · SOURCE

	HOME GATE	ROAD GATE	BROADCASTING
Brooklyn	$1,790,275	$430,797	$ 888,270
Chicago	793,859	245,986	226,603
Cincinnati	1,488,568	303,566	267,275
Milwaukee	2,603,354	342,443	125,000
New York	1,008,183	300,326	730,593
Philadelphia	1,307,937	237,611	301,630
Pittsburgh	1,254,142	240,381	158,500
St. Louis	1,296,226	277,521	327,450

AMERICAN LEAGUE · SOURCE

	HOME GATE	ROAD GATE	BROADCASTING
Baltimore	$1,277,613	$194,334	$ 301,630
Boston	1,610,291	321,654	477,300
Chicago	1,305,125	306,847	518,992
Cleveland	1,326,214	336,400	1,053,171
Detroit	1,433,528	194,334	403,245
Philadelphia	1,702,959	183,415	210,000
New York	2,606,689	498,830	900,000
Washington, D.C.	564,610	207,457	316,640

When attendance was the principal source of revenue, keeping pace with large-market teams was a challenge for the smaller clubs, but one that aggressive management could meet. Teams in the smaller cities have shown to this day how to maintain an adequate gate. The Milwaukee Brewers, to take one example, have routinely outdrawn the Chicago White Sox in recent years until nostalgia for the old Comiskey, fascination with the new stadium, and an exciting young team put Chicago ahead. A look at the rank of cities in population and attendance shows that ticket sales are not the source of the revenue problem for the smaller cities.

137

THE DIAMOND REVOLUTION

Cities Rank In Population
And Attendance, 1990

AMERICAN LEAGUE			NATIONAL LEAGUE		
ATT'D.	CITY	POP.	ATT'D.	CITY	POP.
1	Toronto	*	1	Los Angeles	2
2	Oakland	4	2	New York	1
3	California	2	3	St. Louis	14
4	Boston	7	4	Cincinnati	23
5	Baltimore	18	5	Chicago	3
6	Kansas City	24	6	Pittsburgh	19
7	Texas	8	7	Philadelphia	5
8	New York	1	8	San Francisco	4
9	Chicago	3	9	San Diego	17
10	Milwaukee	25	10	Montreal	*
11	Minnesota	16	11	Houston	10
12	Seattle	15	12	Atlanta	13
13	Detroit	6			
14	Cleveland	12			

*Canadian cities not listed in the U.S. Census list of metropolitan statistical areas.

A competitive team and aggressive marketing will draw people to the ball park in any major league town. At the same time, a huge population base is no guarantee that fans will pay to see a poor club that has been indifferently sold. The responsibility for the gate thus falls to each team, and each front office can be confident that if it does its job, it will keep pace with the other clubs as far as attendance is concerned. Radio and television is quite another matter. The importance of revenues from those sources has raised a series of issues that have been very difficult to resolve, and the future of baseball promises even more intractable problems.

The most urgent issue for many clubs is the tremendous range in local radio and television revenues. In fact, one can say that the so-called "small-market problem" is precisely a problem of broadcast revenues. In 1989, the New York Yan-

138

kees struck a local television deal that realized the fears of clubs like the Brewers and the Mariners. Despite being at the bottom of the Steinbrenner years, the Yankees used their cachet and the New York market to secure a local cable contract with the Madison Square Garden Network (MSGN) that will pay half a billion dollars over twelve years.

Every year before counting the gate, taking its cut of the network contract, and selling its hot dogs, beer, and souvenirs, the Yankees franchise can count on $40 million of revenue just from cable. Combined with radio and over-the-air broadcasts, the Yankees take in more than half of what every other club in the major leagues *combined* receives from local television and radio income. Their receipts are greater than those of the entire National League.

When the national network money that is evenly distributed is combined with the local television and radio contracts, the total media revenue is allocated as follows:

Total Media Revenue In Baseball—1990[2]
(in millions)

AMERICAN LEAGUE		NATIONAL LEAGUE	
New York	$69.4	New York	$38.3
Boston	34.1	Philadelphia	35.0
Toronto	28.0	Los Angeles	29.7
Texas	24.6	St. Louis	27.4
Chicago	24.2	San Diego	25.1
California	24.0	Houston	24.2
Baltimore	22.5	Chicago	24.2
Detroit	22.3	San Francisco	23.3
Oakland	21.2	Cincinnati	21.8
Cleveland	20.0	Pittsburgh	20.0
Minnesota	19.6	Atlanta	20.0
Kansas City	19.0	Montreal	20.0
Milwaukee	19.0		
Seattle	17.0		

In the hunt for media revenue, the Yankees are obviously off by themselves. The Mets, Red Sox and Phillies form the next tier, about half the Yankees' purse. The Dodgers, Cardinals, and Blue Jays crowd $30 million. The White Sox, Angels, Rangers, Padres, Astros, Cubs, and Giants are huddled at about $25 million. The other twelve major league teams receive about $20 million from media sources.

The size of these respective markets is obviously an important factor in the varying media receipts, but it is not the only one. Why, for instance, do the Red Sox make so much more than either the Cubs or the White Sox? Why do the two Chicago teams make the same as the Houston Astros? Why do the Dodgers make significantly less than the Phillies? Why do the Braves report revenues of only $20 million when their games are carried over a national cable superstation? The answers have to do with the media strategies of each franchise, the metafinance of baseball accounting, the performance of the clubs, the economic circumstances of local stations and advertisers, and, not insignificant, the quality of front office operations at each ball club.

The disparity in these revenues fuels one of the dire prophesies of modern baseball. In this apocalyptic vision, the richer teams will be able to corner the best players by paying salaries that poorer franchises cannot match. Walter O'Malley feared the Milwaukee Braves for that reason even when the reserve clause kept salaries on a very short leash. Since free agency has sprung five-year veterans, the prophecy has become more plausible, but it is far from fulfilled.

The Yankees and the Phillies have proved that money buys neither love nor championships. The Pirates, Reds, A's, and Twins have won titles despite their membership among the media poor. The Mariners have managed to be bad on the field and financially strapped, while the Dodgers and the Red Sox have made money and won.

The lament from the small-market franchises is that they may have been able to assemble a great young team, but they will be unable to hold players like Bobby Bonilla once they become free agents. Of course, if clubs cannot afford to keep a prospective free agent, they can always trade him for prospects or try to secure him to a long-term deal before his free agency season. Those moves assume some risk, the kind of thing that most businesses have to do in this country every day.

Some businesses have a recourse. Their risk can be diminished through the protection of a patron, specifically the government. To secure this consideration, a firm must be wealthy, powerful, and considered indispensable to the community—an apt description for major league franchises. The current example of this governmental bounty is called the Major League Baseball Equity Act of 1991.

The measure was introduced by Senator Slade Gorton, a Republican from the state of Washington. The senator's office rejects the suggestion that the bill should be subtitled the Mariners' Relief Act, but the measure is clearly part of the strategy to keep the team in Seattle.

The key provision of the bill would require clubs to split the revenue from the media transmissions of their home games by giving 20% of those receipts to the league for an even distribution among the rest of the clubs in that league. The transmission of road games would put 20% of those receipts in the treasury of the club that had made the deal, with the 80% balance going to the league office for another even split with the other clubs in the league.

Senator Gorton's office has published its estimates of the effects of a fifty-fifty division of revenues between the team securing the contract and the pot to be divided with the rest of the league. This formula is used because "figures from an 80%–20% home and a 20%–80% road split are unavailable but are likely to be similar to those of a 50%–50% split."[3] (See table, page 142.) The expressed objective of the legislation is "to create equity within Major League Baseball."[4] This goal is advanced as a solution to the alleged problems of economic stratification and competitive advantages.

THE DIAMOND REVOLUTION

Estimates of Sharing 1990 Media Revenues and Difference by
Team from the Current Formula (in millions)

AMERICAN LEAGUE			NATIONAL LEAGUE		
New York	$47.8	−21.6	New York	$32.0	−6.3
Boston	30.1	−4.0	Philadelphia	30.3	−4.7
Toronto	27.1	−0.9	Los Angeles	27.6	−1.9
Texas	25.4	+0.8	St. Louis	26.5	−0.9
Chicago	25.2	+1.0	San Diego	25.4	+0.3
California	25.1	+1.1	Houston	24.9	+0.7
Baltimore	24.3	+1.8	Chicago	24.9	+0.7
Detroit	24.2	+1.9	San Francisco	24.5	+1.2
Oakland	23.6	+2.4	Cincinnati	23.7	+1.9
Cleveland	23.0	+3.0	Pittsburgh	22.8	+2.8
Minnesota	22.8	+3.2	Atlanta	22.8	+2.8
Kansas City	22.5	+3.5	Montreal	22.8	+2.8
Milwaukee	22.5	+3.5			
Seattle	22.2	+4.2			

On the merits, the problem with Gorton's proposal is that it cannot identify specific harm caused by the stratification and the advantages. Conceivably, a few clubs could be threatened with bankruptcy at some point in the future, as several have been in the past. At the present time, the pinch that a few clubs feel might require new owners but not necessarily an overhaul of the financial structure of the media money. In fact, the tremendous increases in revenues for owners and players should mean that baseball enjoys a wider cushion than ever, one that could be squeezed considerably before structural changes become imperative.

Another substantive problem with the revenue-sharing formula in this bill is that it changes very little in terms of the problem that allegedly exists. The Yankees would still be richer than anyone else, though not by so much. The tiers would still exist, though the gaps between them would narrow. Why would the Yankees give up more than $21 million

142

a year for any reason, let alone marginal boosts for a dozen teams? Any attempt to force such a plan on the Yankees would almost certainly land the major league owners in an internecine lawsuit with little chance of success.

Perhaps most serious, the plan shares the same problem that most welfare programs have: it cannot discriminate between those who genuinely need some assistance and those who want to ride on the backs of others. While some rough relationship may exist between the size of markets and media revenues, a similar crude connection might link those revenues with the skills and energy of the front offices.

A second media problem that will become more acute in the future is the viewers' access to the game. When fans watch games that are broadcast over the air, they necessarily depend on teams, leagues, and stations to determine which games those will be. The power of the fan is limited to turning on a set and selecting the station that is showing the games that networks, sponsors, and teams have decided we should see. Our choices are to watch that game, another program, or nothing at all. But technological progress has given fans much more power to participate in the decision of what games will be watched.

From the time the first game was telecast (a doubleheader between the Dodgers and the Reds from Ebbets Field in 1939), viewers were the passive recipients of the tastes of those who brought us the games. For twenty years, it was quite enough for most fans to own a television set that would let them assume that passive role.

Cable had been introduced in the early 1950s to carry UHF (ultrahigh frequency) broadcasts to television sets that were blocked by permanent interference. The economics of this technique was simple enough when applied to sports. In traditional broadcasting, stations paid the clubs for the rights to broadcast their games, and advertising spots were then sold to cover the rights fees and turn a profit for the stations. These

UHF broadcasts are often described as free TV, because they do not require a fee for the viewing. If we can resist the inducements of the advertising, we can skip paying even indirectly for the program.

The first direct restriction to watching the broadcast was to scramble the UHF signal. The viewer was thereby forced to rent a descrambler to see the desired program. This new source of revenue could produce a predictable stream of revenue, and it did not necessarily preclude additional income from commercials. This contrived restriction never quite caught on, but it did anticipate that some programs, especially some sporting events, were popular enough to limit to people who were willing to pay for the privilege.

Cable offers several ways to sell games to viewers. As part of a basic subscription, a cable company offers a team's games as one piece of the several stations that comprise the cable package. The broadcaster then makes money two ways: through the subscription fees and through commercials that are sold to sponsors. Having a source of revenue independent of sponsors is a tremendous advantage to cable companies and a potentially fatal limitation for broadcast networks.

Cable revenues can be further enhanced by charging an additional fee beyond the basic cable rate. This tiering of programs recognizes that some shows are so appealing that the public will pay extra to see them. The potential for gimmicks with tiering extends to the limits of the imagination. Programs can be lumped together, forcing consumers to buy unwanted products to secure the only one they desire. Basic cable rates can be low, with high fees charged for special programs, or the rate can be high, with low charges for the most attractive shows.

Tiering has caused battles between cable operators and cable networks. The operators provide the hardware that wires the house and brings the basic package of programs to the viewers. The networks produce those basic programs that will appeal to a wide audience as well as the shows that will attract a narrower following. The basic package includes the twenty-four-hour news of CNN, and the more specialized channels range from the Disney Channel to the Playboy Channel.

Baseball can fit any of the programming categories of television. Some games are best suited for the network telecasts. A local team's home games are good for cable because that coverage is less of a drag on the gate. If the team is especially popular, the market might bear an additional charge to see the games.

The Yankees' local cable deal was complicated by a dispute between the cable network Madison Square Garden (MSG) and the local operator, Cablevision. To cover the cost of the contract with the Yankees raises a simple question: Do you put the games in a basic package and increase the fee for every subscriber; or do you restrict the games to those who are willing to pay the surcharge for a tiered program? MSG succeeded in tiering the cable games but defused the issue by selling some of its games back to WPIX, the Yankees' over-the-air broadcaster.

Of course, nothing necessarily prevents commercials from being shown on programs that already have generated a basic cable fee and a surcharge. One restraint on such commercials is a fear of a consumer rebellion. Movie audiences in California have been known to become restless when commercials are shown before a feature film. This impatience may also assume a political dimension—the voter may feel that enough is enough, that too many middlemen have their hands out for a service that used to be free.

The spread of television itself and cable systems causes some people to think of broadcasting as a necessity of life and one that should be available to everyone. (See table, page 146.) Representative Peter Kostmayer of New Jersey introduced a bill in the 102d Congress titled the Fairness to Fans Act of 1991. This legislation addresses a decision of the Philadelphia 76ers of the NBA to put all their games on cable, depriving,

THE DIAMOND REVOLUTION

Percentage of U.S. Homes With Television and Cable Services[5]

YEAR	TELEVISION	BASIC CABLE	PAY CABLE
1950	9%	0%	0%
1955	67	0.5	0
1960	86	1.4	0
1965	95	2.3	0
1970	96	6.7	0
1975	97	12.6	0.2
1980	98	19.9	6.8
1985	98	42.8	25.7
1990	98	56.4	29.5 est.

among others, voters in Kostmayer's district of free access to those games.

Kostmayer relies on the "universal service" principle in the 1934 Federal Communications Act for his belief that the public is entitled to watch sporting events on television, free of charge. The congressman was supported in his opposition by Comcast Corporation, a large cable operator in Philadelphia. The cable operators are concerned that some of the cable networks are going to charge the operators fees that will have to be passed on to annoyed customers. The operators are also concerned that Representative Kostmayer and his colleagues will draft even more stringent regulations for the cable industry.

Senator John McCain of Arizona has offered similar legislation in the senate. The Public Access to National Sporting Events Act expresses several "findings," some of which are quite remarkable. The bill acknowledges at one point that "many consumers have benefited from the constant availability of sports programming through subscription media."[6]

The bill then states, "Nonetheless, the access by members of the public to certain sports events should not be dependent upon their ability to pay." The senator thereby enters dangerous territory.

146

He relies on a civic religion view of sports, one that is significantly different from accepting sports as a business that should operate in a market. By elevating sports to a moral plane above other businesses, McCain inadvertently encourages a conceit about sports that has been thoroughly corrupting. If the polity will suffer without the games (the evident assumption behind McCain's finding), then the games must be preserved at virtually all costs. This is precisely the attitude that has led communities to build stadiums for ball clubs, that has confused universities about the true missions of their athletic department, and that is consistent with the irrational impulses that have caused some athletes to destroy themselves with steroids.

The bill starts to make a useful point in some ensuing findings, but it draws the wrong conclusion. The World Series is one of the events that is singled out for exemption from the normal requirement of a market economy: the ability of the consumer to pay for the product. McCain notes that the Series, and other events, are enormously popular in part because of support that the public has provided through Congress and the courts.

He specifically mentions the antitrust exemptions that have facilitated the negotiations over broadcast contracts. Because such public policies have contributed to the prosperity of professional sports, McCain asserts that the "American tradition" of the World Series should "remain available to the public via live broadcast television."[7]

These concerns were poignantly mentioned in an article by media expert Curt Smith in the *Sporting News*. Smith recalled his ninety-year-old grandfather, who lived in a small upstate town in New York. The old gentleman had watched NBC's "Game of the Week" for so many years that the broadcast had become an old friend. Smith championed the interests of his grandfather and others who love baseball for its simple pleasures.

In a similar vein, in the Philadelphia 76ers case, a local

147

paper warned that "the gentrification of professional sports television is upon us."[8] The editorial invoked also the civic religion perspective by recalling the importance of sports in inspiring children to be the next great athlete: "The dream may be a 10 million–to-1 shot, but it is better than dreaming of buying the silver Mercedes owned by the local drug dealer."

This hysteria about the games lends some credibility to a delightful farce in *Sports Illustrated* that describes a future world of television, including Welfare Sports Aid and Sports Aid stamps for the less fortunate who are unable to afford pay-per-view.[9]

This compassion for the fan who does not have modern equipment is a great concern for the cable industry because they fear the political steps that compassion might inspire. Their reply is that cable and satellite communications have made significant numbers of games available for public viewing that previously went unseen. Their figures claim that from 1985 through 1989, the number of major league games shown on cable grew from 820 to 1,061, while the number of free games broadcast over the air climbed from 1,536 to 1,647.[10]

New technology will give viewers even more choice about what games will be watched, albeit at a price. The trade-off for consumers having control over what game they see is that a satellite dish will have to be purchased or a cable subscription will be needed.

Politicians may assert that the new technology is problematic for the public interest, but what they should consider is whether the largesse that professional sports receives should be continued. Treating baseball franchises as businesses rather than parishes in the civic religion would promote a far healthier public climate for sports. Then individuals could make their own decisions about whether or how much they are willing to spend to see the World Series or another event.

* * *

Technology is also changing access to the games in a way that makes one of baseball's most settled policies about radio and television an anachronism. Rooting for the home team is not only a baseball lyric, but it has been a pillar of the game's economy, a pillar that is now cracking. Transmitting baseball games has turned on the principle of stay out of my market and I'll stay out of yours. But changes in broadcasting technology have already given clubs the means to present their games in one another's markets, and very soon individual fans will have the means to decide for themselves what games they want to see regardless of league considerations.

While the major league owners have been unable to determine where competition ends and collegiality begins with broadcast revenues, technology may force them to an even more radical step: sharing markets. Throughout the refinement of cable systems and their development as important telecasters, the primacy of geographic markets continued to determine the economic decisions. Fans who subscribed to cable systems had a few more choices of games to watch, but the protection of local teams from electronic competition remained a dominant consideration in major league baseball.

The last serious challenge to that nostrum was the building of superstations, networks that carry the games of one team to virtually every community in America. Superstations came to baseball in 1976, when Ted Turner purchased the Atlanta Braves. His fellow owners thought Turner had renounced any intentions to take his local Atlanta station national, but Turner changed WTCG into WTBS and began to hustle the Braves as America's Team. America largely resisted the Braves until 1991.

Turner effectively prevailed over the owners who opposed him as well as over Bowie Kuhn, who as commissioner carried the banner for major league baseball against the interlopers from cable. Kuhn and Turner battled in virtually every arena of government, with a few victories for the commissioner but without a serious threat to the steady advance of cable.

149

THE DIAMOND REVOLUTION

In 1985, Peter Ueberroth was hired by the baseball owners to become commissioner because they assumed he would bring to the job the business skills that the game desperately needed. In their choices for commissioner, the owners had previously selected a federal judge, a politician, a sportswriter, a general, and a lawyer. Ueberroth was the first commissioner to know at least as much about running a business as the owners themselves.

As a peer, he told them that they were doing a terrible job of running their clubs. His most famous legacy was the owners' collusion against free agency, but he reinforced another anticompetitive impulse of the owners by striking at the superstations. To Ueberroth, these networks represented chaos in what had been stable markets. The benefits of stability were the monopolistic advantages that each club held in its local market and the collective monopoly of major league baseball in negotiating its national radio and television packages.

If the monopoly were replaced with a market, as the traditional argument went, winners and losers would ensue with the winners using their wealth to outbid the losers for free agents, to scout and develop superior prospects, and to market their clubs more aggressively, thus extending the competitive advantage. The old specter of a prosperous few dominating the game has persuaded the owners to behave themselves.

This fear of the market has strong roots in American capitalism, especially among the wealthy. The great trusts of the Gilded Age in the late 19th century were born of an abhorrence of chaotic markets. J. P. Morgan, John D. Rockefeller, Andrew Carnegie, and the several railroad barons were appalled at the waste and duplication in competitive markets. Price wars, ventures into untested communities, and the prospect of new rivals militated against planning, control, and the certainty of future revenues.

When we think of planning and regulating in business now-

150

adays, we associate it with government control, but the old robber barons, including those in baseball, saw it as something else. They intended a self-regulation, a fraternal control of the erratic impulses that might strike an individual. The common good was thus preserved against the indulgence of individualism run amok. Indeed, the old fraternity of owners embodied just such values.

These two themes have battled to define the nature of American business: the free market based on individual self-interest versus a monopolistic control that promised order and stability. Teddy Roosevelt and the Progressives were not so much enamored of government as they were opposed to the concentration of power in a small elite of the wealthy and privileged. Their antitrust laws and the subsequent litigation were aimed at returning American business to the boisterous uncertainty of a market economy.

Baseball's antitrust exemption is as much a symbol as a cause of this industry operating by the standards of Morgan and his friends. Ueberroth and the majority of owners reacted to Ted Turner the way old money reacts to the nouveau riche. The new commissioner required that the interloper pay a tribute to the barons of the invaded territories. The payment has been adjusted periodically, and to this point the super-stations have been stabilized.

By itself, the technology of cable is little more than a substitute for over-the-air broadcasts that are interrupted by mountains or other sources of interference. What potentially changes everything about the politics, economics, and mechanics of watching baseball is the introduction of satellite transmissions.

Satellites have been a part of broadcasting and cable for many years. Television and radio transmissions may be sent from a stadium to a satellite transponder that redirects the signal to a receiving station that in turn sends "the pictures, descriptions, and accounts of the game" to fans' televisions and radios.

The equipment that has been needed to receive the broadcast signal from its original source or the transponder has been rather enormous in size and expense. In the way of modern technology, that is changing dramatically.

Receiving dishes the size of dinner plates at a cost of $200 will be available in a few years. Less obtrusive than an aerial, the dishes will enable a fan to aggressively pursue the signal of the game of her choice. Once that signal is in the air, it can be picked off by anyone with the technological means to do so, and those means are becoming increasingly accessible to viewers in their homes. To be blunt, games that have been withheld from fans because the grand strategy of networks and leagues has dictated another choice will be stolen by fans if a sensible way to pay for the product is not made available.

The most likely reaction of major league baseball is to scramble the signal to prevent the theft. In conjunction with scrambling will come a stern warning about the fines and imprisonment that await the thief who has stolen a Mariners-Royals game. But chances are good that descramblers will find their way to market, and it is very doubtful that loyal fans who stole a game simply to see "their" team will be marched off to jail. Even fines would have to be applied carefully to prevent Major League Baseball from appearing as a bully.

This freewheeling market with a touch of Robin Hood is far from the construction that the major leagues apply to media transmissions. Commissioner Fay Vincent continues to defend the traditional importance of local markets.[11] He draws an analogy between major league teams and McDonald's franchises. When the golden arches are planted in one locale, another McDonald's franchise is not allowed in the territory.

The analogy to McDonald's is too narrow, because the more germane comparison is to the fast-food industry as a whole. If a McDonald's is established on one corner of an intersection, a Burger King is likely to join the neighborhood, along with an Arby's, and the other fast-food chains. And so the Giants are different from the Cubs who are different from the Orioles who are different from the Red Sox who are different from the Astros, and so on. Distinctions among teams' uniforms, stadiums, locales, and styles of play are the very factors that cause us to be fans of one team instead of another.

As hungry diners, we choose among pizza, chicken, hamburgers, and barbecued ribs in the same neighborhood. Those are the choices that will be coming to fans in their living rooms. A menu of every game will be available for the selection of the individual fan whose television will become incomparably more powerful in conferring choice on its owner.

The implications for the major league clubs are staggering, and they seem as yet unprepared for them. The preference for the security of safe local havens will become irrelevant. Whether local broadcast money is shared or not, fans will decide to breach the barriers of technology that have restricted communities to local clubs. The home team will doubtless remain of paramount importance to most fans, but other clubs will be important alternatives.

Some of the franchises may pursue a strategy of building an especially attractive team and marketing it across the country. The Oakland A's could use Jose Canseco to appeal to Hispanic fans in Florida and Texas. The Astros, the Rangers, and the Marlins might not be happy about that, but such an incursion may be the only way for the A's to pay for Canseco's next contract.

During the 1960s, the most popular team nationally in the National Football League was probably the Green Bay Packers. The legendary club included dramatic personalities from Vince Lombardi to Paul Hornung, and their exploits were followed all over the country. If some similar dynasty were built in baseball, many fans might want to pay to see such a club at least occasionally.

A less troubling change for baseball is the way we will be watching the games. Andy Dolich is the vice president for marketing of the Oakland A's, and he offers an intriguing view of the future of baseball telecasting.[12] The viewer will control the picture much as a television director now does. At the pressing of a button, the images from perhaps fifteen to twenty microcameras present the options that the fan has for watching the game.

The cameras will be so small that they can be placed in the pitching rubber, home plate, and other strategic locations. One can imagine an aging third baseman content to watch an entire game from the perspective of the hot corner while safely ensconced in a lounge chair.

The opportunity for instant replay from a dozen cameras would entertain the fan, if not the umpires. Electronics and microcameras could hold the strike zone constant despite the differences in leagues, the girth of umpires, or a laugher in late innings on a hot afternoon.

Conceivably, cameras could be located on the players themselves, as is now done in the World League of American Football. Further miniaturization might be required, but that kind of progress is virtually inevitable.

This kind of intrusion by the fan into the game itself is a part of what is known as interactive television. This extraordinary technology will transform the way we use television, and it is forcing all the current powers that be to scramble to find a niche in that new world.

Dolich foresees a day when a marketer's dream will come true. A fan will be watching the A's in a tight struggle with the Red Sox. Just after Jose Canseco hits a decisive home run that wins the game, the screen flashes a question: Do you want to see the Red Sox on the A's next home stand?

You pick up a small hand-held selector and reply. Assuming you do want to see the Sox, the screen asks you where you want to sit and how many tickets you want. You punch in the information (your credit-card number is already known by the machine), and something like a fax machine instantly presents you with your tickets.

As Dolich says, "That's the way to sell tickets." The sale is made in the heat of the moment. The fan does not have to make a phone call, let alone drive to a ticket booth. Delay is eliminated, and attendance rises.

When the fan gets to the park for the Red Sox game, he will find that each seat includes a small computer screen. If he chooses, the fan can participate in the game by predicting what the next play will be. One inducement to play will be competition among the fans at the stadium as well as fans watching at home. Points could be awarded for the fans who correctly predict home runs, strikeouts, and double plays. The points could then be applied to prizes such as tickets to a future game, team jackets, and autographed baseballs.

As the technology of broadcasting and cable becomes ever more dazzling, one of the greatest threats to the baseball business is a proposed restriction on the sponsoring of these games. The financial foundation for baseball transmissions is beer. Companies like Anheuser-Busch put significant amounts of money into the treasuries of each of the major league franchises in return for the chance to sell their product and to advertise at the stadium and on the team's television and radio transmissions. The present financial structure of the game, including player salaries, could not continue if the breweries withdrew from baseball.

For that reason, efforts to restrict the free hand of the beer companies to sell their product are a potential financial disaster for baseball. In that regard, the breweries face two threats. The first is that drinking becomes unfashionable. Concerns about health could lead to the linking of alcohol with tobacco—substances that should be avoided in the interests of avoiding disease. Per capita beer consumption is already declining in this country, perhaps a result of an aging baby boom population.

Discussions of alcohol that compare the product with drugs or tobacco are vehemently challenged by the beer industry. Steve Burroughs, a vice-president of consumer awareness and education for Anheuser-Busch, counters that illegal drugs and tobacco are products for which there is no responsible use.[13] Beer, on the other hand, can be safely consumed if it is used according to directions. Specifically, it should be consumed in moderate amounts by people who are not alcoholics, and no one who is driving a car or performing any other task that could lead to death or injury should drink on those occasions.

To the industry's critics, that position ignores the unique appeal that alcohol has especially to young people, who may not be influenced by the rational encouragement to be responsible. The critics' concerns have found a political voice, and that is the second problem facing baseball and the beer industry. Legislation has been introduced in Congress that would require health disclaimers in broadcast commercials, a step that could cause Anheuser-Busch and the other breweries to pull their ads from television and radio—an economic disaster for baseball.

The health warnings that are being proposed are very similar to the ones that appear on cigarette packages. A bill introduced in the second session of the 101st Congress in April 1990 by Rep. Joseph P. Kennedy calls for one of the following warnings:

Surgeon General's Warning: Drinking during pregnancy may cause mental retardation and other birth defects. Avoid alcohol during pregnancy.

Warning: Alcohol impairs your ability to drive a car or operate machinery.

Warning: Alcohol may be hazardous if you are using any other drugs such as over-the-counter, prescription, or illicit drugs.

Warning: Drinking alcohol may become addictive.

Warning: It's against the law to purchase alcohol for persons under age 21.[14]

The problem for the breweries is less the message of the warnings than their effects on the commercials. The Kennedy bill calls for the warnings to be read on all audio ads, "in an audible and deliberate manner and in a length of time that allows for a clear understanding of the health warning message by the intended audience."[15]

Similarly for televised ads, the warnings must be included in a "graphic representation" in which "all letters in such health warning appear in conspicuous and legible type that is not script or italic, that such health warning be surrounded by typographic lines that form a box, and that such health warning appear in the same length of time as is required for the reading of the message."[16]

Whatever those requirements mean—and lawyers could have a field day with them—the beer industry thinks they mean that the advertisement that costs a significant amount of money is being trashed. The industry points out that it currently sponsors ads that call for the responsible use of alcohol, but it insists that two separate sets of commercials are necessary to keep the messages clear. Including the health warnings with ads that present beer in an attractive way defeats the purpose of the ads, the industry believes, and removes any reason for running them.

Burroughs is optimistic that the legislation will not pass, but it is noteworthy that the bill that is sponsored in the House of Representatives by Joe Kennedy is sponsored in the Senate by Strom Thurmond. Those two names rarely join on anything, and their taking similar leadership positions means that diverse interest groups agree on this issue.

Joining Kennedy and Thurmond is Rep. John Conyers from Michigan, a black member of the House, who pointed out in his testimony that the African Americans are the focus of ad campaigns of the tobacco and alcohol industries that make those products the two most heavily advertised in black neighborhoods. Conyers had been an original sponsor of the legislation.

THE DIAMOND REVOLUTION

Representatives from various treatment centers for drug and alcohol abuse testified in favor of the bill. Adding his voice to theirs was Monty Roberts, a former Busch Beer brand director. Roberts left his prominent position within Anheuser-Busch to become a Christian lay minister with special responsibilities for drug and alcohol treatment.

Other religious figures testifying for the bill were Robert Parham, associate director of the Christian Life Commission of the Southern Baptist Convention and Bishop Felton May of the United Methodist Church Council of Bishops Initiative on Drugs and Alcohol Abuse and Violence.

Further support for the bill came from the American Medical Association (AMA), the American Academy of Pediatrics, and the American Academy of Family Physicians.

The beer industry received some support from the American Civil Liberties Union (ACLU), which found provisions of the Kennedy bill to be an unconstitutional abridgement of commercial free speech, but Steven Shiffrin, a law professor at Cornell University and a leading authority on the First Amendment, expressed the view that the bill was constitutional.

Whether these groups are correct on the merits of their arguments is not the point here. Of significance for the business of baseball is that such a broad coalition has been assembled to support a measure that would threaten the broadcast revenues of every team.

In his testimony against the Kennedy bill, Edward Fritts, president and chief executive officer of the National Association of Broadcasters, asserted:

To require warning labels to be a part of alcohol ads will simply drive those ads off the air without achieving the goal of reducing alcohol abuse in America. Advertising is the only source of revenue which broadcasters have. The impact on the ability of broadcasters to provide public service to their community—including news and public affairs as well as sports and entertainment programming—will significantly diminish if this bill becomes law.[17]

Other opponents of the bill, including James Sanders, president of the Beer Institute, claim that the problem of alcohol abuse is unrelated to advertising and that the bill would not solve the problem that it addresses. Sanders also believes that if the health warnings are required, the beer companies will pull their spots.[18]

Congress might never pass such a bill. If they do, the president might veto it. If the bill were passed and signed into law, courts might strike it down on First Amendment grounds. But the political sources that are supporting health warnings are impressive. A coalition of the AMA, Southern Baptists, a black congressman, Joe Kennedy, and Strom Thurmond is remarkable on its face. They may never win on this issue, but an industry would be foolish to bet its future on it.

The future of media transmissions seems to be that any fan will be able to see any game that she wants. Technology permits that now, but the financial and legal barriers to using the equipment are still formidable. The cost of the cable systems and dishes is likely to drop to become accessible to most households. The legal barriers will either have to adjust to these new realities or become anachronistic.

Nowhere in all of the changes in baseball has so much power been put in the hands of the fan. Owners wring concessions from politicians. Players raid the owners' treasuries for millions of dollars. Soon the fans too will have the object of their desire: they will be able to watch their favorite team whenever it plays, whether the league, the networks, or the commissioner's office wants them to or not.

The future will also include international broadcasts. Some teams now send radio accounts to Mexico if a player like Teddy Higuera is on the mound. Revenue from these transmissions is negligible at this time; but if baseball develops as an international sport, the income from sending televised games back to every country represented in the major leagues is potentially enormous. A World Series that includes international competition could be followed the way World Cup soccer currently attracts fans.

The technology of broadcasting seems to be limited only by imagination. If the economic issues can be resolved, the future of baseball, for the fans, will be truly spectacular.

NOTES

1. Congressional hearings, op. cit (p. 103, n.1).
2. Anthony Baldo, "Secrets of the Front Office: What America's Pro Teams Are Worth," *Financial World*, July 9, 1991, pp. 42–43.
3. Data from News Release, Senator Slade Gorton, September 19, 1991.
4. Ibid.
5. Figures from *The Universal Almanac 1991*, pp. 240–41.
6. S1015, 102nd Congress, 1st Sess., 1991.
7. Ibid.
8. *Philadelphia Inquirer*, July 11, 1991.
9. William Oscar Johnson, "Sports in the Year 2001," *Sports Illustrated*, July 22, 1991, pp. 40–48.
10. "Fair Games: Broadcast and Cable Coverage of Televised Sports," *Issues in Brief* 1, no. 3 (December 1989).
11. Vincent interview.
12. Andy Dolich, interview, Dolich's office, August 23, 1990.
13. Steve Burroughs, interview, Burroughs's office, September 13, 1990.
14. H.R. 4493, 101st Cong., 2d sess., 1990, p. 6.
15. Ibid, p. 8.
16. Ibid, pp. 8–9.
17. Written testimony of Edward O. Fritts, president/CEO, National Association of Broadcasters, on H.R. 4493, July 18, 1990, pp. 1–2.
18. James Sanders, interview, Sanders's office, August 3, 1990.

7

Baseball
and Booze

The potential loss of beer money from television and radio sponsorship is only one of the challenges that baseball faces from alcohol. The treatment of players who may have a drinking problem has been a persistent issue for front offices. Combined with new concerns about losing players to AIDS, the need is ever more acute to find policies that respect players' privacy while pointing out the perils that threaten them.

Through the history of baseball, alcohol abuse has claimed some prominent players:

• Ed Delahanty, the greatest power hitter of the nineteenth century, died in 1903 at the age of thirty-five. He fell drunk into the Niagara River and was swept over the Falls.

• Grover Cleveland Alexander battled alcoholism while winning 373 games in a brilliant twenty-year career. He survived until 1950 when, at the age of sixty-three, he died alone, drunk, and ignored in a rooming house in a small Nebraska town.

• Bob Welch fired a third strike past Reggie Jackson for one of the memorable moments in World Series history. Welch is not likely to join Delahanty and Alexander in the Hall of Fame, but he may have made a greater contribution than either of the immortals. In discussing his alcoholism and his turn to a sober life, Welch stripped an ugly disease of its glamorous veneer.

Baseball mythology is full of stories of boozing ballplayers whose physical gifts enabled them to play heroically even when blind drunk or hung over. The stories are so enthralling that serious questions about the players' health seem almost alarmist, and the point is nowhere clearer than in the case of the game's greatest player.

The many elements of Babe Ruth's legendary career are outside our immediate concern. The question here concerns his drinking and the reaction to it of his employer and the rest of organized baseball. Ruth was neither the first nor the worst of baseball's drinkers, but his notoriety as a boozer sometimes matched his fame as a hitter. Forty years after his death, it would be lurid and pointless to chronicle his famous drunks. But if Ruth had a problem with alcohol, his treatment will tell us a lot about baseball's attitude toward drinking.

In Robert Creamer's superb biography, Ruth's drinking is discussed at several points. "He could drink extravagant amounts of liquor, and he got drunk a lot and raised hell, especially in the early years. . . . Yet, when he had to, he could discipline himself, and he had a continuing sense of responsibility to certain people and certain things, among them his own position as Hero."[1] Ruth's ability to pull back from booze when things were getting out of hand distinguished his reputation, if not his health, from that of Grover Cleveland Alexander. Old Pete could rarely leave the bottle alone.

In 1921, Ruth got into an argument in a Prohibition roadhouse. When the Babe left to go home, the man he had sparred with followed him, forced Ruth to pull his car over, and confronted him with a gun. Several teammates arrived to rescue Ruth from what could have been a fatal scrape.

In his retirement, the Babe became an avid golfer. Creamer writes that Ruth would have four or five drinks at lunch before a round and a couple more at the turn. The consumption on the nineteenth hole is not reported.

Creamer concludes with the testimony of Ben Curry, who ran the Leewood Golf Club and who played frequently with Ruth. The Babe would stop at Curry's house and down half a quart of Scotch before heading for the course. Curry's testimony is that Ruth was not an alcoholic because he could switch to soft drinks whenever his liver flared up from too much liquor. Only after his liver recovered would the Babe resume his old ways.

Because Ruth could moderate his drinking periodically, he did not fit the most familiar pattern of alcoholism, but it is fair to ask why a healthy person would return to drinking something that had damaged his liver. More to the point, clinical questions about Ruth's drinking can muddle a simple fact: the man endangered his life and his career through reckless behavior that included excessive drinking.

Part of Ruth's legend is that he performed so well despite the abuse his body endured. Indeed, any damage that his indulgent living did while he played is hard to document. In his last full season, at the age of thirty-nine, the Babe still hit twenty-two home runs and batted .288.

He missed a significant number of games only in 1925, the year of the Great Bellyache. As a young man, the Babe was an incredible physical specimen who seemed relatively unaffected by his intimate knowledge of at least four of the Seven Deadly Sins. But his retirement was burdened with apparent heart trouble and then his fatal bout with cancer. The game's greatest hero died at fifty-three.

How did the Yankees brass handle Ruth's drinking? About as well as could be expected at that time. The Yankees were then owned by Jacob Ruppert, who grew up mixing an aristocratic life-style with manual labor in his father's brewery. After four terms in the U.S. House of Representatives and an active life among New York's swells, Ruppert invested part of his fortune in the New York Yankees.

Ruppert knew his limits, which included no experience in baseball. He hired brilliant executives like Ed Barrow and George Weiss to run the franchise while he reigned over the fledgling dynasty. During the 1920s and 1930s, Ruppert saw the Yankees develop into the preeminent franchise in American sports.

Periodically, Barrow and Yankees manager Miller Huggins tried to pull in the reins on their wayward star. Ruppert never failed to back up his manager and front office against the showdowns that Ruth provoked. The Babe was treated as a wild youth who needed discipline imposed since none was to be found in his own makeup. Modern treatment programs for drinking were unheard of in the 1920s and 1930s, so the options for anyone disposed to help Ruth were limited. Given the realities of the time, an occasional crackdown on Ruth's worst behavior was probably as enlightened a strategy as was possible.

The one bad season in Ruth's career was 1925. He began the year with a serious intestinal problem that was ascribed to his excessive eating, drinking, and carousing. Surgery was needed to cure an abscess in his stomach, and he missed the first part of the season. When he returned, he challenged Huggins's authority to set curfews for the team and was fined and suspended for his outbursts.

Faced with united opposition in the Yankees front office, Ruth backed down and apologized to Huggins in front of the entire team. The episode chastened him as far as that was possible, and he began the most productive period of his career at the age of thirty-one.

The Babe's hard drinking has been celebrated because it did not appear to interfere with his game and because he always seemed to be having such a good time. In contrast, Grover Cleveland Alexander was clearly suffering, especially when he returned from World War I, during which combat had aggravated both his epilepsy and his drinking. The young man from

Nebraska who had arrived in the majors so kind and innocent spent the rest of his life in a torment of illness and humiliation.

Alexander had unbelievable numbers before going to war.
He came up in 1911 and won twenty-eight games as a rookie.
He had 192 wins before leaving for France in 1918, an average
of twenty-seven wins per year. He pitched for another twelve
seasons after returning, but he won more than twenty games
only three more times. Where Ruth drew crowds simply by
walking down the street, Alexander was such a painful sight
that he was avoided.

Old Pete's most legendary performance as a player came in
the 1926 World Series, in which he faced Ruth's Yankees.
Inevitably, his drinking became central to the story. Alexander won the second and sixth games, squaring the Series both
times. Leading 3–2 in the seventh inning of the seventh game,
he was brought in to face Tony Lazzeri with the bases loaded
and two out.

As the story goes, Alexander was loaded himself after celebrating his win in Game Six. Some reports claim that manager Rogers Hornsby had to meet Pete in left field to help him
to the mound. Although drunk or hung over depending on
the version, Alexander struck out Lazzeri and held the Yankees at bay in the eighth and ninth innings to secure the
championship for the Cardinals.

The legend is disputed by Les Bell, the Cardinals third
baseman, in Donald Honig's *Baseball America*.[2] Bell insists
that Alexander had been moderate the night before because
Hornsby had told him he'd be in the bullpen for the seventh
game. Bell further denies that Hornsby met Pete anywhere
but on the mound. The strikeout was the result of a brilliant
pitcher using his guile to outwit an eager rookie.

While Ruppert handled Ruth like an aging Huck Finn, Sam
Breadon, the Cardinals owner, treated Alexander as a charity
case. Money from the Cardinals, disguised as a pension, was
sent to Pete for the rest of his life. But the stipend was not

sufficient to keep Alexander from appearing in a 42nd Street sideshow, where the curious could see what had become of one of baseball's greats. As Breadon saw it, Alexander simply could not stay off the bottle, so he was an object for sympathy and charity.

Looking at baseball and society as they were before World War II, the owners who felt responsible for Ruth and Alexander did reasonably well by the two of them. Ruppert disciplined the Babe, and Breadon gave charity to Pete. Different treatments would probably be prescribed today, but within the limits of their time, Ruppert and Breadon did not do badly.

After the graceful reign of Joe DiMaggio, another boisterous era loomed for the Yankees in the 1950s.

"I remember one time he'd been injured and didn't expect to play, and I guess he got himself smashed. The next day he looked hung over out of his mind and was sent up to pinch-hit. He could hardly see. So he staggered up to the plate and hit a tremendous drive to left field for a home run. When he came back into the dugout everybody shook his hand and leaped all over him, and all the time he was getting a standing ovation from the crowd. He squinted out at the stands and said, 'Those people don't know how tough that really was.' "3

The hero of this familiar tale is Mickey Mantle. He joined the Yankees in 1951, DiMaggio's last year in baseball. Mantle was the next great Yankees slugger, continuing the tradition that began with Ruth in 1920. He combined the Babe's love of a good time with DiMaggio's reluctance to let the press and public know him too well.

Mantle joined with Whitey Ford and Billy Martin for some memorable forays into New York nightlife, and club officials were again challenged with handling a wayward star. The Ruppert strategy was dusted off after Yankees owners Del Webb and Dan Topping received a bill from a nightclub where the lads had been celebrating their clinching of the 1953 pennant.

Unsure of how to split the tab, Ford suggested having it sent to the club and paying for it later. The brass was not amused, and Mantle and Martin were summoned by General Manager George Weiss. As Mantle describes it, "We rushed to the Squibb Building on Fifth Avenue—Yankee headquarters—sat down in the outer office, and waited an hour. We sat there like two truants from grade school, waiting to be sent in to see the principal—the guy with the paddle."[4]

Weiss began the counseling with a tirade and a $1,000 fine for each player. He then sent them to Dan Topping, who had them wait another hour before advising them that he could send them to jail for forgery. The fines were reduced to $500 apiece, and they were forgiven entirely after the Yankees beat the Dodgers in the World Series. The episode is a great example of unabashed paternalism. No doubt the players acted like adolescents, but the reaction of the Yankees brass was at least as immature.

What was the point of demanding an immediate appearance, then forcing the players to wait for hours? No reason except intimidation. Why not simply call the players to tell them to send the money and not to bill the club again? No reason except that one would treat a peer that way, not an underling. Why threaten players with jail for forgery when such charges would have been a joke? No reason except that Mantle was gullible enough at the time to believe his boss.

In the case of the Yankees, paternalism crossed the line to a contemptuous arrogance. The purpose of Weiss and Topping was not to inform the players of club policy or even to reprimand them for their presumption. The object of the Yankees executives was to belittle the players and remind them of their place.

The most notorious episode during this period occured in 1957, when Mantle and several other Yankees went to the Copacabana to celebrate Billy Martin's birthday. The players had an argument with another party, and before the fisticuffs could begin outside, one of the hecklers was knocked out. The Yankees were hurried outside before police and press could arrive, but the news was in all the papers the next morning.

George Weiss, his limited patience at an end, traded Martin to the Kansas City Athletics a short time later. Tolerance for boozing was an easier policy for the superstars than for the mere mortals, but even Mantle was routinely reminded of the Copa incident during contract battles.

Before Martin left, he and Mantle got drunk and pushed the good times close to a tragedy. As Mantle sets the stage, "One night in Detroit, after we had dinner and hit a few bars, we got up to our room drunk, looking for something to do, just to be ornery. I think we were staying on the twenty-second floor.

"I can't remember whether it was Billy or me who had the bright idea, 'Hey, let's climb out on the ledge and see what we can see in the other rooms.' "[5]

The voyeurism ended at the next room, where the lights were out. At that point, Mantle rediscovered a fear of heights, and he was unable to turn around on the narrow ledge. He and Martin had to crawl completely around the hotel to get back to their own room.

At one point in the narrative, Mantle implores, "Don't ask me now why I did it." No need to ask. They were bombed, and they risked their lives to play Peeping Tom. If your most valuable employee could take that kind of a chance when he drank, what should you do about it? The Yankees' solution was to break up the social club by shipping Martin to Kansas City.

One of the players whom the Yankees received for Martin was Ryne Duren, a wild, hard-throwing relief pitcher whose thick glasses added to a batter's unease. Duren was another of the hard-drinking Yankees, but for Mantle there was a critical distinction about Duren, a recovering alcoholic.

Baseball and Booze

"I used to run around with Ryne a lot. But, thank God, I was lucky enough to have had a greater tolerance or a stronger stomach. I don't know. As I've said elsewhere, I got into the habit of drinking heavily—especially in the off-season—quite early in my career. First beer, then the hard stuff."[6]

Mantle writes that he has restricted his drinking to social occasions since his wife was injured in a serious car accident caused by his drinking. But he still reflects the common attitude that an alcoholic lives in a different world from that of a heavy drinker. Duren is associated with Pete Alexander while Mantle is linked with Babe Ruth. Many employers share that attitude—as long as the worker can perform, whatever goes on outside the workplace is a private matter.

In baseball, if a player could arrive at the park and do his job, then the club could ignore his drinking. Ruth and Mantle seemed unimpaired as players, so the club disregarded their drinking as long as they didn't challenge team officials or create a public embarrassment.

Suppose a player's drinking is approached differently. Look at whether a player endangers his life, his health, and his career through behavior related to his drinking. From that perspective, the Yankees would have had good reasons to be concerned about both Ruth and Mantle. For humanitarian and business reasons, the club might well have wanted to deal with these players more seriously.

Baseball's traditional requirement had been a simple one: Drink the bars dry, go to bed with every woman in town, just be ready to play. If you're a superstar, we'll be even more tolerant. You cannot challenge the authority of club officials, nor can you embarrass the franchise, especially if you can be easily replaced. But if you can pull back from the bottle as the needs of the game and the club require, then as far as we are concerned, you have no problem with alcohol.

Bob Welch and the Dodgers dumped this old standard. For all of its elegance and apparent respect for privacy, in some cases the old policy was a formula for disaster. Ball clubs, along with other businesses in America, were learning by the 1970s that problems with liquor cost lives, cut productivity, and diminished earnings whether the drinker technically qualified as an alcoholic or not. The new concern of business has been to salvage people before their luck runs out.

This new strategy came along just in time for Bob Welch. Born in Detroit in 1956, Welch grew up in a working-class home where drinking was taken for granted. He played several sports in high school and had already begun to drink heavily. In college at Eastern Michigan University, Welch developed impressive reputations for pitching and for drinking.

On a college All-Star team touring Japan, Welch kicked in some hotel doors and performed the apparently obligatory walk on the ledge. The antics drew the attention of Rod Dedeaux, the great coach of the University of Southern California who was managing the all-stars. Dedeaux told Welch that he was acting "just like an alcoholic," the first time anyone had confronted Welch about his behavior.

Welch recalls, "Dedeaux was telling me that the problem went deeper, more than just having a couple of beers. He could see that my personality changed when I drank, that I abandoned all pretenses at being civilized. He could see there was a troubled human being inside that crazy kid heaving bottles off a building."[7]

Baseball was slow to recognize that emotional pain can cause people to destroy themselves. Dedeaux's intervention was unusually thoughtful and perceptive, but since he and Welch were together for a short time, the talk did not have a lasting effect. Welch soon returned to his old ways, but his pitching stayed sharp enough to attract the Dodgers, who drafted him in 1977.

He made it to the majors the following year, won seven games to help the Dodgers win a pennant, and struck out Reggie Jackson for the final out of the second game of the

World Series. The next season promised more glory in a brilliant career, but it delivered more chaos for a life that was out of control.

By being drunk on the field before a game at Candlestick Park in September 1979, Bob Welch crossed one of the lines of the traditional policy on alcohol—he had embarrassed the club. The club reacted in the time honored way: Welch was fined $500 and chewed out by manager Tom Lasorda and general manager Al Campanis.

Breaking with tradition, the Dodgers kept tabs on Welch during the off-season. Even though there were no dramatic episodes, club management invited Welch to Los Angeles in January to give him the opportunity to begin a treatment program for alcoholism.

Peter O'Malley, the Dodgers owner, is a board member of the Union Oil Company. After learning of Union's Employee Assistance Program (EAP) for alcoholism and drug treatment, O'Malley had a similar program set up for the Dodgers, the first EAP for a sports franchise.

Bob Welch was the first player to recover through such a program. He entered a treatment center in Arizona and announced during spring training in 1980 his decision to live a sober life. Recovery from his disease can be measured only on a daily basis, but one day at a time Welch has enjoyed good health ever since. And the career that he salvaged culminated in a Cy Young Award in 1989.

In some ways, Welch was an ideal candidate. He was good enough to attract attention and concern, but not so famous that he might have been too embarrassed to admit his problem. His decision to cooperate with the team in getting help for his problem is not as colorful a story as Mantle on the hotel ledge or Alexander fanning Lazzeri, but it has been an important inspiration for other players who have needed help.

Since alcohol does not discriminate, its problems befall club executives as well as players. Larry MacPhail went on some notorious benders while presiding over the Brooklyn Dodgers just before World War II. Horace Stoneham, the owner of the New York Giants, was believed to follow the policy that the sun was over the yardarm somewhere in the world. If club officials, players, umpires, or anyone else in baseball has a problem with alcohol, he can now get help.

Perhaps the key to the new treatment for alcohol abuse is the appreciation by the owners and players that they share a common interest. Saving a man's life and salvaging a career transcend narrower concerns, and baseball is significantly better for that realization.

Because drinking is both legal and popular in polite society, determining when an individual has a problem can be difficult. The related problem of drug use is somewhat easier to define, because any use of a proscribed list of drugs can be grounds for action. The 1991 suspension of Otis Nixon and the arrest of Steve Howe are the latest in an apparently diminished but persistent string of players with drug problems.

The Players Association and the owners have not been able to formulate a policy to keep the game free of drug problems, and one could conclude from some of their differences that the owners favor a tough course while the union favors leniency. That distinction is overly simplistic. The owners hate to lose a player like Steve Howe, who has great talent and who represents a tremendous investment in player development. The union and the owners fell out over the issue of testing, a practice that may or may not be part of an effective policy of drug treatment and prevention but which certainly evokes the bad old days of George Weiss bullying the Yankees.

The owners need to be wary about using the drug issue as a way to reassert control over the players. And the union needs to be careful not to "protect" the player into a fatal relapse. Part of the pattern of abusing either drugs or alcohol is the denial of the problem. Both the employers and the union have to keep uppermost in mind that a life is in jeopardy and could be lost if it is treated as another issue in the long battle between labor and management.

Perhaps because of persistent efforts to educate players about the risk of drugs, the number of cases has declined in the past few years. Magic Johnson's revelation of his HIV infection may further encourage players to be more circumspect about their private behavior. But one of the great risks that will not go away is the players' belief in themselves as people with gifted bodies who can overcome problems that break mere mortals. As long as those beliefs remain focused on the game, the athlete is relatively safe; but if they extend to personal conduct, more tragedies may await.

Developing effective policies about drinking is not easy for baseball, because alcohol is a menace with one redeeming feature—it is the foundation of some of the game's great fortunes. Jacob Ruppert was only one of the owners whose wealth depended on booze. Chris Von der Ahe, a saloon-keeper, set the mold back in the nineteenth century when he built the St. Louis Browns of the American Association into the best team of its time. In recent years, baseball's preeminent beer master has been August Busch, Jr.

Born in 1899, Gussie Busch took over the family business in the mid-1940s, inheriting the Anheuser-Busch breweries that had been established in 1861. Busch was cut from some of the same cloth as Jake Ruppert: having inherited fortunes, neither was reluctant to enjoy life.

Busch acquired a reputation as a sportsman, which meant that he liked to fish and hunt, could handle a drink, and could tell a story or two. Among his companions on the hunting trips were Stan Musial and Red Schoendienst, friends even though Busch hadn't attended a Cardinals game in years.

In 1953, Cardinals owner Fred Saigh was imprisoned for tax violations, and the Cardinals were ripe for a sale that could have taken the club from St. Louis. Since the Browns had already left for Baltimore, the city faced the loss of major league baseball.

Motivated, it is said, by civic pride, Busch purchased the Cardinals for $3.75 million. Whether through calculation or dumb luck, the combination of a brewery and a ball club was a breakthrough in the modern business of baseball. The Cardinals became as great a marketing device for Budweiser as the Clydesdales. The team, in turn, has enjoyed a financial base that few clubs in baseball can rival.

In an article for the *Saturday Evening Post* in 1957, Busch described his early days as a baseball magnate. Among his initial surprises was how much more attention the public paid to the Cardinals than to the brewery. When Dick Meyer was appointed a vice president of Anheuser-Busch and also general manager of the Cardinals, the brewery job received passing attention in the business press while the sports pages devoted columns to his post with the ball club. Busch was amazed because the Cardinals were worth about one-tenth the value of the brewery.

For Busch, the Cardinals were a new toy. He wrote that he tried not to interfere with those who'd been hired to run the club, but he reserved a "fan's" right to second-guess. He compared the Cardinals with other recreations. "I still love to feel a strong horse under me and listen to the bugling of the stags. I still thrill to the recoil of a good hunting rifle in my hands and the sight of a flight of geese across the sky. But there's no thrill for me today like seeing my team come from behind to win with a run in the ninth inning."[8]

This life of baronial splendor floated on an ocean of suds that poured through the taps of saloons all over America. The bottles and cans of Budweiser that trucks delivered from coast to coast represented the foundation of a life that few in their bars and dens could imagine.

In a few more years, Busch, the country squire, would be introduced painfully to the 1960s and new attitudes about labor relations. His players, who were overpaid by the standards of the 1950s, demanded fair pay by the standards of a competitive market. One of his stars, Curt Flood, sued baseball to overturn the antitrust exemption rather than permit the Cardinals to trade him to Philadelphia. During this more turbulent era, when Gussie Busch bugled the stags, they stopped answering.

In 1964 and 1967, the Cardinals won world championships to fulfill Busch's great ambition for the team, but the simple joys of baseball were diminished. During the 1964 season, at a point when the Cardinals seemed out of the race, manager Johnny Keane learned that he would be replaced at the end of the year. When the Cardinals rallied to take the pennant and the World Series, Busch called a news conference to announce a new contract for his manager. Keane had an announcement of his own: he was quitting.

The shocking departure of Keane followed a midseason firing of Bing Devine, the general manager who had put the championship team together. Busch's chagrin at driving out the men who had brought him a championship was followed in the 1960s and 1970s by bitterness over the new militancy of players.

Busch personified the paternalism of the old Tory owners. He genuinely cared for his players and saw them as peers in certain respects. His admiration for Stan Musial has been unqualified, and Musial remains an executive with the Cardinals today. For Busch, the Cardinals were an extension of his family and he was the head of the clan.

From Busch's perspective, the rise of the Players Association was a slap in the face. By the end of the 1960s, Busch was publicly accosting the players for their greed. Had he not been generous to his boys all those years? Why did they now want a commercial relationship with salaries totally out-of-bounds with what the owners could afford?

His perspective was sincere but completely out of touch with the times. During a period when the most basic social and economic assumptions were challenged, Busch wanted to maintain the status quo. Perhaps he assumed that nature knew what it was doing when it appointed people to their respective stations.

For some of the major league owners, the challenge from the players was threatening but impersonal. Bill Veeck truly did not have the money to play the major league game under the new salary scales. Walter O'Malley had the money, but he made no bones about his reluctance to part with it. For owners like Busch, the new relationship was not only economically unwise, but, worse, it was a personal betrayal.

Gussie Busch played a central role in driving Bowie Kuhn from the commissionership, but the episode was his last major activity as one of baseball's power brokers. In the 1987 World Series, Busch ceremoniously drove the Budweiser carriage, Clydesdales and all. Until his death in 1990, he retained the titles chairman of the board, president, and chief executive office of the Cardinals. But the reality is that the Cardinals have passed to corporate ownership.

Busch's son, August III, took control of Anheuser-Busch in the early 1970s, although he apparently lacks his father's enthusiasm for baseball. Fred Kuhlman has come over from the brewery to run the ball club, indicating that the Cardinals may now be more a marketing device for A-B than a hobby for the Busches.

Kuhlman himself is emphatic that the Cardinals are run separately from the brewery.[9] He insists that the ball club must be a profit center for the parent company. The Cardinals have undoubtedly been so, drawing annual attendance that is matched by only a few clubs in far larger markets.

An internal study by the Cardinals has shown them that half their fans at the park are women, 20% are children, and 45% of the weekend crowds are from out of town. Kuhlman ascribes the team's popularity to the fact that the teams are consistently good and the stadium is operated to attract families.

176

Baseball and Booze

Bud Selig is in a unique position to assess the influence of Anheuser-Busch in baseball: he has the only major league team in the United States that doesn't sell or advertise Budweiser.

If anyone is under the gun of Anheuser-Busch, it would be Selig. The Brewers play in a small market just 100 miles north of Chicago. Broadcasting revenues are limited, and Selig's financial base outside of baseball is limited to automobile dealerships—a modest resource by baseball standards.

Selig may be the most popular and respected owner in baseball, and, in his opinion, Anheuser-Busch has "bent over backward" to avoid even the appearance of using its wealth to bludgeon baseball clubs.[10] He says that the brewery is "extremely sensitive" to the charge that it dominates baseball through the power of beer. Selig includes A-B among the more responsible owners of ball clubs.

The brewery's behavior has been especially significant in the past fifteen years. During the 1970s, after being acquired by Philip Morris, the Miller Brewing Co. challenged Anheuser-Busch by developing the first sophisticated, and occasionally sophomoric, ads targeted at sports fans.

Under August Busch III, Anheuser-Busch developed a modern marketing strategy to repel the threat from Miller. By competing directly for the sports dollar, A-B and Miller saturated sports programs with appeals to drink beer. By associating drinking with jocks, the breweries pandered to the sexual insecurities of young men   a certain path to wealth if ever there was one.

Through aggressive bargaining, Anheuser-Busch sought and received some contractual advantages, including the "right of first refusal," which gives the holder of a current contract an opportunity to match any bid by a competitor for future contracts. Since A-B was the largest brewery to begin with, this legalized inside track guaranteed that A-B lost only those contracts that it didn't mind losing. As long as a ball club wants to sell beer, the chances are good that it will be selling the beer of its colleague and competitor A-B.

177

THE DIAMOND REVOLUTION

When the dust settled in the beer wars, Anheuser-Busch had won in a rout. The brewery now sells more than 40% of the beer that is consumed in the United States, while Miller sells about 20%. If present trends hold, A-B will eventually control half the American domestic beer market.

Begin with Anheuser-Busch's size, add the ownership of the Cardinals, plus contracts with twenty-three major league teams, plus the explosion of sports marketing, plus first refusal rights, and warning bells sound.

Despite Bud Selig's assertion that Anheuser-Busch has been responsible, the brewery has had its lapses. In 1984, A-B paid $2 million in a consent decree to the Bureau of Alcohol, Tobacco and Firearms settling charges that it had strong-armed sports stadiums to sell only A-B's products.[11]

The allegation against Anheuser-Busch accused the brewery of a classic antitrust action—the attempt to establish a monopoly in American ball parks. While it is true that baseball enjoys an exemption from antitrust law, the exemption doesn't extend to breweries, and baseball itself doesn't need this kind of publicity.

The account in the *Wall Street Journal* risked little adverse publicity because it was brief and buried. In the classic resolution that large corporations use with the government, Anheuser-Busch claimed to have entered the consent decree to prevent long proceedings. It added that the agreement did not mean that the brewery was guilty of the charges, but the alleged actions were not company policy, so the offensive behavior would stop. In exchange, further investigations by the government were dropped.

With potentially so much to lose, it makes sense that Bud Selig is right—that Anheuser-Busch is extremely sensitive to the impression that it might be a corporate bully that corrupts baseball. The charges from the government most likely stemmed from the misdeeds of a few zealots rather than from a willful corporate policy. Still, it makes great sense to remain wary of Anheuser-Busch. A corporation of that size, wealth, and power has advantages in dealing with the government that the rest of us do not enjoy. The private firm may well have more resources than the government, so the ability of the state to protect the public interest against corporate mischief is limited.

The company also displayed its enormous influence in wresting control of Busch Stadium in St. Louis. The ball park was constructed in a public-private venture during the 1960s, and it was then run by the Civic Center Redevelopment Corporation. In 1981, the brewery tried to buy the stadium to secure the concessions and parking revenues.

Civic Center resisted the takeover. It even filed suit, contending that Anheuser-Busch had used insider information in its bid for the property. At one point, the brewery suggested that if it were unsuccessful, it might move the Cardinals from St. Louis.[12] The threat was credible because 7-Up emerged as a potential white knight for Civic Center and 7-Up is owned by Philip Morris, the corporate parent of the Miller Brewing Co.

Within a week, the suit was dropped, and after a few months of wrangling, the brewery had itself a ball park. The cost of the hostile takeover had risen from A-B's initial bid of $33 million to a final price of $56 million.

For corporations like Anheuser-Busch, a free market is an ideal competitive arena. Given its advantages going into any contest, A-B is a likely winner against commercial or civic adversaries, so corruption such as bullying the stadium vendors is worse than illegal, it is embarrassing and unnecessary.

Baseball has had to face other problems related to alcohol. One of the most serious threats comes from drunks in the stands who can turn a game into a nightmare, such as the one in Cleveland in 1974. In the ninth inning of a game between the Indians and the Texas Rangers, hundreds of spectators stormed the field, causing a forfeit in what had been a tie game.

The riot culminated an evening of rowdy behavior that was fueled by an irresponsible promotion of ten-cent beer. Twenty-three thousand fans were served 65,000 ten-ounce cups of beer at ten cents a cup. The Rangers bullpen had to be evacuated earlier in the game, and during the chaotic ninth inning an umpire was hit with a bottle.

Nothing so violent has occurred at a game since, but no team has been so foolish in its promotions. The chaos since the Cleveland episode has been more mundane. Isolated fights and offensive displays are common at ball games, and they are tolerated to a point by both the public and the clubs.

A spontaneous outburst from an excited fan can be part of the fun of going to a game, but the constant aggravation of a few drunks can ruin the enjoyment. To alleviate problems caused by drunken fans, Techniques for Effective Alcohol Management (TEAM) has been employed since 1985 by professional teams in all sports. The techniques include training for stadium vendors in identifying patrons who've had enough. Another phase of the program is directed at fans who are encouraged to moderate their own behavior. TEAM has had some success in its first few years, and that coincides with changes in public attitudes about drinking.

Alcohol-free sections have been established at many stadiums. Restrictions on vending beer in stands and ending sales after the sixth or seventh inning are other measures that clubs are using to eliminate the nuisance and dangers of excessive drinking. Any loss of revenue from these restrictions may be overcome by greater attendance from fans who simply want to enjoy a ball game rather than become part of the show.

The new policies about drinking are a more honest attempt to balance the inevitable conflicts about alcohol. In the past, baseball tried to have it both ways: responsible drinking was encouraged, but, after all, these are real men who play the game, and real men occasionally get bombed. If some fans followed suit, they might have been asked to quiet down or leave, but their money would have been gratefully counted. The costs today of that old approach in lost players and potential lawsuits are more than a sensible business will want to accept.

Alcohol and baseball will always be associated, and the owners who rake in so much money from beer have a special obligation to be responsible to their players and fans. Employee Assistance Programs and TEAM are two examples of progress from the days of Mickey, Billy, and Whitey.

Both players and fans at the ball park are more likely to find alcohol taken seriously by the club. If the new policies are enthusiastically enforced, lives will be saved and careers will be salvaged. If the policies become little more than public relations gimmicks, then baseball will return to scenes of desperate players and rowdy fans.

The remaining area for improvement is media advertising. The rational plea to drink moderately pales in the subliminal context of Drink More! Since sports marketing inevitably focuses on young men, special consideration needs to be taken of their limitations. Any appeal to the brain is likely to be no more effective than if it were addressed to a spawning salmon, so the same techniques that advertisers use to attract young men to their product should be used to warn of its dangers.

As long as one receives the message that beer equals champion athletes equals sexual prowess, those ads will trigger excessive drinking. Breweries and ball clubs have recognized their self-interest concerning their players and their paying customers. The same regard for the viewer at home is the next logical step.

Alcohol, often described as a drug, can also be thought of as a food—one that some people are allergic to, and one that anyone can overdo. If our culture lionized shellfish or strawberries as the path to manhood, the incidents of intestinal distress and hives would skyrocket. We celebrate alcohol in just that way, and it can kill.

Owners and players have found a mutual interest in alcohol control that is encouraging. By facing the problem, the suffering of players and the annoyance to fans has been eased. If this new attitude can influence the advertising of beer, then the century-old riddle of how baseball should handle booze will be closer to a solution.

NOTES

1. Robert Creamer, *Babe: The Legend Comes to Life* (New York: Simon & Schuster, 1974), p. 21.
2. See Donald Honig, *Baseball America* (New York: Macmillan, 1985), p. 158.
3. Jim Bouton, *Ball Four* (New York: World, 1970), p. 30.
4. Mickey Mantle, with Herb Gluck, *The Mick* (New York: Doubleday, 1985), p. 107.
5. Ibid, pp. 162–63.
6. Ibid, p. 176.
7. Ibid, pp. 67–68.
8. August A. Busch, "Baseball's Got Me!" *Saturday Evening Post*, May 18, 1957, p. 128.
9. Fred Kuhlman, interview, Kuhlman's office, September 13, 1990.
10. Bud Selig, interview by telephone, August 10, 1989.
11. *Wall Street Journal*, June 25, 1984, p. 41.
12. *Wall Street Journal*, June 19, 1981, p. 27.

8

The Workers
Arise

When the Shah of Iran was teetering on the Peacock Throne,
he often called Washington, D.C., for advice. The conversa-
tions were pointless, for the ailing despot was at endgame, far
past the point at which accommodation would have been welcomed by his subjects or repression been effective. The Shah
found himself in the position of so many others, like Louis
XVI, Nicholas II, and Bowie Kuhn.

The major league owners were in no danger of following the
fate of earlier tyrants. To the contrary, the players were delighted to have the owners make more money than ever. As
revenues grew through licensing, broadcasting, and greater
attendance, so salaries would skyrocket. The owners have
come to see that a gaping hole has been ripped in their purse,
and their increased revenues inevitably pour into the players'
pockets. And in their more honest moments, they surely must
realize that the breach in their treasuries was largely self-
inflicted.

The stunning rise to power of the players and their union is
a fairly familiar story, but its lessons are still in dispute, so the
future of labor relations remains clouded. A review of the
history of the owners' treatment of players shows not occasional blunders but a flawed perspective that triggers a pat-

tern of behavior that has backfired drastically. If the owners think they simply have to be a little sharper in the future, they will repeat the mistakes of their past. They must instead accept the truth that they are barons no more and that they will either share power with the players in making all the major decisions that they face or their money will continue to fly to the players' pockets.

They must also face the reality that almost everything that they predicted about the effects of the players' gains have been proven wrong and everything the union promised about those gains has been proven correct. The owners predicted financial ruin, but the greatest prosperity in the history of the game has occurred since free agency was introduced in 1976. The owners predicted championship dynasties by the few wealthy clubs, but, as the first chapter showed, the competition for pennants has never been greater. Both the game and the business have dramatically improved, and, like it or not, the owners can thank their bitter adversary.

The first flaw in the owners' perspective is their fortress mentality. Even when they ruled the game alone, they saw the world as Us and Them. Happy Chandler's language about the Pasquel brothers or the prospect of a players strike reflected not just opposition but indignation. George Weiss's patronizing treatment of his wayward stars was hardly the way someone would treat a peer. Branch Rickey's condescending dismissal of Ralph Kiner's salary request—"We could have finished last without you"—showed that the blind elitism reigned in the most progressive front offices.

A fortress mentality inevitably produces one damning characteristic: those in power do not listen to those whom they rule. As the owners routed Danny Gardella, George Toolson, and Curt Flood in the courts, they failed to hear the essential legitimacy of the players' claims. Secure in technical legal points of *stare decisis*, the owners were blind to justice.

The indifference of the game's rulers to the complaints of players who made less than $10,000 per year was a gratuitous offense that Marvin Miller was able to exploit. Many players then, like many blacks in the game now, were angry about their circumstances, and the owners did not recognize or respect that fundamental grievance.

Commissioners and other executives appeared before congressional committees during the 1950s to defend the reserve clause and the antitrust exemption. They were successful in the sense that Congress took no action to reverse the 1922 Supreme Court decision. But they failed to realize that the antitrust exemption would not square with mainstream American attitudes about fair commercial practices.

The failure to listen caused two more problems, the first of which is the narrowing of options. The choices in running baseball's business necessarily were limited to decisions that conformed to the owners' values, especially the value of maintaining their own comfort. Since the treatment of players as chattel had been sustained by Congress and the Supreme Court, why start thinking of more fair and prudent interpretations of the reserve clause?

The second problem of not listening is the blind assumption that the way things are is the only way they can be. The preservation of the status quo becomes the objective of every institutional endeavor. People who warn about potential problems or who express the grievances of those suffering at the moment are dismissed as alarmists or radicals.

When Sandy Koufax and Don Drysdale bargained before the 1966 season as a tandem, with an agent, for a contract that would have paid the two of them about a million dollars over three years, they were completely beyond the pale. The least of the objections from the Dodgers front office was the money. What was completely out of line at the time was using an agent, asking for a multiyear deal, and bargaining collectively.

For the 1965 season, Koufax had been paid $85,000 and Drysdale $80,000. At that time, no one received multiyear contracts, and a $100,000 salary was like beatification before canonization at Cooperstown. No pitcher then had a salary in six figures, and only Mickey Mantle, Willie Mays, Stan Musial, and Ted Williams had been paid above that financial benchmark.

So secure were the rulers of baseball that when Koufax and Drysdale exercised a holdout, the only option for a player who would not accept the terms proposed by his club, the Dodgers brass was delighted. In his memoirs, Buzzie Bavasi, the Dodgers general manager, recalled his final offer before spring training. Together, but not as a formal package, the two stars would get $195,000.

> They declined, and the Great Holdout officially began. So had
> spring training, sans Koufax and Drysdale, whom I maintain to
> this day we could have signed in a minute. But there wasn't
> any reason to sign them. The holdout was making headlines in
> every paper in the Los Angeles area every day. I explained
> this to Walter O'Malley who as well as anyone understood the
> value of publicity.[1]

This case is one of the great examples of the labor climate in the mid-1960s. The dispute centered on a simple question: what was their value? The greatness of the two pitchers hardly needs to be mentioned, yet the Dodgers could define that value unilaterally because the players were trapped regardless of their talent. The reserve clause in those days reached even in Asia, so when Koufax and Drysdale threatened to play in Japan, Bavasi remembered, "I found [that threat] amusing." What would send a general manager into apoplexy today could then be dismissed with a smile.

The tone of the negotiations is worth noting. Bavasi writes, "At no time were there any harsh words from either party. It never got ugly."[2] Drysdale's account of the episode is candid about the ways in which Bavasi tried to con Koufax and him into thinking that what each had been asking for was way out of line with the other's request—the realization that they were being played against each other precipitated their joint negotiation. But Drysdale concludes, "I always had the highest

186

respect for Mr. O'Malley and Buzzie, and our brief separation in the spring of 1966 didn't change a thing."[3]

Most remarkable is Drysdale's sentiment that "strangely enough, I felt sorry after it was all over for Mr. O'Malley. We had put him in an uncomfortable spot with all his peers."[4] Drysdale clarifies that his concern was not financial—he had no doubt that the O'Malley treasury was still intact. But he was aware of O'Malley's standing among the other owners and that breaking the $100,000 mark with two pitchers from the same club was unprecedented.

This compassion for O'Malley is important. If one were asked to complete a triumvirate of sensitivity that begins with Alan Alda and Phil Donahue, one would not pick Don Drysdale; yet Drysdale was able to think about the negotiations from O'Malley's perspective. One of the toughest pitchers ever to compose chin music could hear the other side, listen to their arguments, see their points even while disagreeing, and examine an array of options. Don Drysdale, who once hit Lou Brock rather than "waste" three pitches walking him, could do all those things, but the major league owners could not.

The Dodgers pride themselves on being a progressive and thoughtful organization, so one would not expect acrimony in their negotiations. But the genteel air suggests that the novel aspects of the Koufax-Drysdale position were so impossible that it posed no threat. An organization that fifteen years later would throw millions at Dave Goltz and Don Stanhouse could face down two of the greatest pitchers in baseball history over a fraction of that money.

A postscript to the holdout is a wonderful illustration of how the business looked from the executive suites of 1966. Bavasi writes, "Reluctantly, we had to admit to ourselves that their ploy worked. Koufax had gotten a $40,000 raise, Drysdale a $30,000 raise. Had they negotiated alone, neither would have gotten that much." Only people totally secure in their invincibility could think that paying players like that an extra few thousand dollars constituted a defeat.

THE DIAMOND REVOLUTION

* * *

The time of the Great Holdout was a pivotal moment for baseball. The 1960s were fully under way, with radical changes in race relations, sexual behavior, music, religion, drug use, family ties, education, dress, speech, movies, and every other social custom and expression. The country was reeling from violence on city streets and college campuses and the random horrors of a few deranged minds. Every institution from the family to churches to business to government was desperately trying to adjust to the new challenges. In the midst of this upheaval, baseball magnates could not have been more obtuse if they had time-traveled from the cabinet of Jefferson Davis. And they were about to reap the whirlwind for their refusal to change.

While the owners were chuckling over or cursing the demands of Koufax and Drysdale, the major league players were being introduced to a candidate to head their association—Marvin Miller. The time to accommodate the rebels was now very short, and the owners, like so many despots, still did not have a clue of what was to befall them.

Miller had two fundamental issues: money and justice. The owners focused only on money, and the players got both. The new head of the union pounded home two points. The first was that players were underpaid; the second, that they lacked the fundamental rights of any American to determine their employer and the basic conditions of their work.

Miller's attack was thoroughly misunderstood by the players and their representatives. Some of Bowie Kuhn's less personal observations focus on Miller's liberalism: "His left-of-center views were deep-seated and pervasive. . . . Miller had a deep hatred and suspicion of the American right and of American capitalism."[5] And in a widely cited observation, Kuhn said, "I began to realize that we had before us an old-fashioned, nineteenth-century trade unionist who hated management generally and the management of baseball specifically." Kuhn added that some of the owners and their practices confirmed the suspicions that the commissioner ascribed to Miller.

Kuhn's successor, Peter Ueberroth, has a more generous opinion of Miller, telling the *Sporting News*, "I think he's an honest, hard-working, dedicated individual. . . ."[6] Ueberroth added that he expected Miller to someday be elected to the Hall of Fame.

Lee MacPhail sounded a similar theme, describing Miller as "a very intelligent, hardworking man with very strong labor instincts and feelings."[7] The emphasis suggests that Miller belongs with the spate of Democratic presidential nominees who get trounced for being unfashionably liberal.

The owners and top officials seem to believe that Marvin Miller sprang at them with a quasisocialist wish list. The irony is that while the owners were worried about Karl Marx, Miller was promoting Adam Smith. Kuhn thought that Miller abhorred American capitalism, but, in a Progressive tradition, Miller simply opposed those capitalists who resisted taking the risks of a market.

In the battle of ideas and values that would soon be joined, Miller had the tremendous advantage of leading a union in a fight for some of the most traditional American notions of how the economy should work. Even as the country began to favor Republican presidents and proclaim itself "conservative" in polls, the Players Association was never outside the flow of public opinion. As labor unions waned in strength across the country, the association won victory after victory.

Leaving the merits of their respective positions aside, Miller and the union were successful because they worked hard, used imagination, took chances, explained themselves to their members, and had a position that was very difficult to assail.

The owners, at the same time, were the embodiment of a bankrupt regime. They fulminated about a possible catastrophe from the higher salaries that they were paying, but the specter was never credible. Even the owners who claimed to be driven from the game by the new salary structure simply sold their clubs at great profit to corporations or entrepreneurs who were better equipped to compete in the more prosperous business climate that the players had created.

During the years of battles between the players union and the major league owners, public attention has focused primarily on the issues that have caused or threatened the playing of the games. Ostensibly, the critical issue that has provoked strikes or lockouts has been something like pension contributions or eligibility of a few players for arbitration. The real cause of the work stoppages has been the effort of the owners to regain control over their business. But there is no basis for believing that the old feudal days will return, so the owners need to think about finally adjusting to the new realities.

The old regime began to collapse as the first Basic Agreement between the owners and the union was reached in 1968. The contract followed two years of work by Marvin Miller to correct flaws in the players' pension system, the task for which Miller was hired in the first place.

After ending some bizarre practices, such as players contributing to their own pension funds, Miller focused on several of the worst abuses of the players. Throughout his discussions, he worked thoughtfully and prudently, realizing that most of the players had no inclination to support a union. The marginal gains of the Basic Agreement of 1968 included an increase in the minimum salary from $7,000 to $10,000 per year, a three-dollar-per-day jump in meal money, and a process for resolving disputes between players and clubs that included using the commissioner as an arbitrator.

Pension issues continued to dominate baseball's labor relations over the next couple of seasons. In 1969, the union encouraged players to hold out until the pension dispute was settled. Miller was dissatisfied with the amount of the owners' contribution to the pension fund and also with the limited access to the money by the players. By requiring a five-year career to be eligible to receive the benefits, the owners had precluded most players from ever drawing a pension. The settlement that was reached just before the 1969 season dropped the eligibility threshold to a four-year career, and it also increased the owners' contribution to the pension.

Miller was entering his fourth season as head of the union, and the owners decided to make a change of commissioners. William Eckhert, a retired air force general, had succeeded Ford Frick in 1965, and whatever his military talents were he was not suited for the demands of the job. The fault was hardly Eckhert's. He was hired to be a figurehead while the owners continued to operate through fraternal consensus. The consensus, however, was proving completely inadequate to the times.

To protect their own interests, the owners needed a sharp, powerful executive to force accommodations in the labor field and head off the team that Marvin Miller was assembling. If the owners had been better attuned to the signs of the times, they would have realized their need for a strong central authority who could seriously reform the way that clubs treated players. That message could not penetrate the owners' psyches because it meant that the Middle Ages were over and the modern era of business had finally come to the grand old game.

The owners' choice of Bowie Kuhn to lead them in the 1970s was a sign that they had not grasped the issues at hand. Kuhn has been caricatured as the preeminent stuffed shirt and company man. In another job at another time, Kuhn would have had a prominent, distinguished career, earning the esteem of his colleagues and acquaintances. But in the commissioner's job during the 1970s, Bowie Kuhn was a public relations disaster.

As with Eckhert, the fault was not really Kuhn's. He worked diffidently to effect some minimal changes on the labor front, but he was bold in challenging owners like Charlie Finley, whose behavior offended the norms of the fraternity. Kuhn's perspective was classic elitism. Like a member of a privileged dining club, Kuhn rigorously guarded the standards of tradition while seeming to be oblivious to the lives of those who prepared the meals.

By the time the new commissioner took his post, Miller had infused some militancy into the players union, and negotiations for a new Basic Agreement began with the union slightly emboldened. The talks have been described as "the least publicized contemporary labor relations activities in major league baseball."[8] They were also the most important.

Again, the minimum salary was raised marginally, and severance pay was increased for players who were cut early in the season. But an adjustment was made in the arbitration process that made this Basic Agreement the most important one ever reached. The commissioner was retained as an arbitrator for charges that concerned "the integrity of the game," but other disputes would now go before a three-member arbitration panel. One arbitrator would be picked by labor, one by management, and a third would be accepted by both sides.

Without impugning the integrity of any of the arbitrators, it is immediately evident that the independent arbitrator is the key figure. The other members would presumably bring to any proceeding policy biases that would heavily influence their consideration of a specific case.

The revolutionary aspect of this agreement is that it removed vital decision making from the culture of baseball. The owners surrendered the power to preserve the status quo without apparently realizing the significance of the step.

In Kuhn's account of the beginning of independent arbitration, he writes:

> While I thought the change was neither necessary nor beneficial, and though it could not have been made without my consent, I reluctantly went along. There had never been a commissioner whose fairness in disputes between clubs and players could be questioned, and if anything they had proba-

bly been more sympathetic to the players' side of disputes. But provisions of this kind were commonplace in American collective bargaining agreements and could not realistically be resisted by sports management—nor have they been. So the clubs and I concurred.[9]

These remarks, written in 1987, do not reflect even the benefit of hindsight. While the *sincerity* of commissioners in their treatment of players might be conceded, their fairness was quite another issue. And by noting that the use of arbitrators was routine in American business, Kuhn should have realized that the pervasive values of business, including the right to choose your own employer within your profession, would inevitably affect the exercise of authority by the independent arbitrator. But even upon reflection, Kuhn seems unaware of that logic.

Lee MacPhail had worked with Commissioner Eckhert, and in his memoirs he notes the decisive blunder:

The clubs should have made absolutely certain—in black and white—that the arbitration procedure had no jurisdiction over their Reserve System. They thought that this was very clear—and, in truth, the arbitration procedure was not supposed to impinge upon this—but eventually there was an arbitrator, Peter Seitz in 1976 [sic; 1975 correct date], who reached out to make a landmark decision in this area and his jurisdiction was upheld by a Federal Court.[10]

Not even the union seems to have been aware at the time how momentous arbitration would prove to be. The issue of the reserve clause was being addressed by a study group representing players and owners, but any negotiated change to the system would have been many years down the road.

Curt Flood's case was another distraction from the significance of the 1970 contract and independent arbitration. The owners could see another challenge to their control through litigation, and they could agree to talk about the reserve clause because that did not herald any change in the system. But the fortress mentality with its inevitable tunnel vision left them blind to the possibility of arbitration ending what the courts, Congress, and contract talks were leaving untouched.

Kuhn writes that he understood the owners' vindication in the Flood case as a temporary achievement. He saw that the court was giving the owners some time to negotiate changes in the reserve clause with the players. The commissioner explored those possibilities but found the owners unreceptive. Kuhn lacked both the institutional power and the personal force to lead the owners through the necessary adjustments. Since modest reform was rejected, radical change became inevitable.

The labor climate became increasingly contentious in the early 1970s. Owners had tired of Miller's victories, and they seemed eager to provoke a confrontation that might disrupt the solidarity of the union. They took a hard line on pension issues in 1972 when that agreement was up for renewal, and the players reacted with the first strike in modern baseball.

A settlement was reached after two weeks of the season were lost. Kuhn and some others were optimistic that the chastening experience would improve the climate for negotiations on the Basic Agreement that would be renewed in 1973. The animosity among the parties continued, and again the players scored a tremendous victory through collective bargaining.

Pension issues were settled along with the Basic Agreement, minimum salaries were increased marginally, and the reserve clause was removed formally from the contract for further study while in effect. But the players stole a march again through arbitration. If a player with two years' experience could not reach agreement on a new contract with his club by February 1, he could take the dispute to binding arbitration.

The owners saw this concession as a moderate step to forestall some of the pressure to end the reserve clause, but they misjudged the issue disastrously. Since the arbitrator must choose either the player's request or the club's offer, arbitration has a universal upward pressure on salaries. Rarely could a club even consider proposing to cut a player's pay and expect to win in arbitration.

Even more significant, the authority to determine a player's value had now radically changed. Up to this point, the only check on an owner's opinion was the pressure of a holdout. Salary arbitration substituted an independent party's opinion for the owner's, and the substitution would be made at the player's request. Conceivably, a player like Johnny Bench could have made the argument that he was worth a million dollars a year, and the arbitrator could have agreed, skyrocketing salaries in a single year. The reality was a more deliberate process for a time, until free agency triggered the dramatic raises that continue to this day.

Salary arbitration made comparisons among players more apparent, and statistics became far more important than the feelings of the front office in determining players' values. Some concern has arisen that on-the-field performance has been influenced by salary arbitration. Will players be so willing to make important plays that do not register in the box score if that lack of a record diminishes their significance in the eyes of the person who determines his salary? No serious evidence has ever indicated that the game has been so diminished, but all the new statistics in baseball could provide fodder for a self-centered game.

Salary arbitration set up one method for determining a player's value, and free agency created another. Andy Messersmith and Dave McNally had the same complaint as George Toolson, Curt Flood, and so many other players about being bound to a club for life. Unlike their predecessors, they had a new forum to vent their grievance. Bypassing litigation, the two pitchers invoked the independent arbitration that the union had secured in the 1970 Basic Agreement.

Convincing federal judges of the illegality of the reserve

195

clause had been unsuccessful because judges bowed to the opinions of their predecessors, opinions whose weight was augmented by congressional inaction. But an arbitrator had a fresh look at the issues and could decide anew whether the team's lifetime hold on players was reasonable.

Peter Seitz ruled on December 23, 1975, that Messersmith and McNally had discharged their contractual responsibilities to the Dodgers and the Expos, respectively, by playing a single option year without a signed contract. The reserve system that had given the owners a stifling control over the players for a hundred years was over, and Seitz was then fired by the owners.

The barons of baseball predicted absolute disaster. Kuhn had feared that Seitz would rule as he did, and he told the owners to fire the arbitrator while they could. The commissioner said that in a world of free agency, he anticipated the collapse of the minor leagues and the possible demise of one of the major leagues.

At this point, Kuhn and MacPhail noted the deficiencies of the old reserve system and the wisdom of reform. They decried the stiff-necked resistance of the owners, who obstinately refused to recognize the need for change. But Kuhn and many of the owners continued to focus on Marvin Miller as the villain in the loss of their privilege. This personalizing of the decision was a further reflection of the fortress mentality, and it only compounded the owners' problems.

A dispassionate look at labor relations in 1976 would have foreseen two problems for the owners. First, the combination of free agency with arbitration would create a powerful ratchet. Owners would determine the market value for free agents, and arbitrators would have that standard to determine the worth of another player. If a single owner paid an excessive salary to a player, the effects could be permanent and universal. The decision to fight about pension contributions and minimum salaries and to reject changes in the reserve system had left the owners blind to the potential force of arbitration. They were now in its vise.

The second problem that the owners should have seen was that they had changed places with the union in terms of the status quo. The owners had always claimed that the game was great as it was and that change was dangerous. Now the owners were in the position of having to force change to save themselves from the union's success.

Neither Marvin Miller nor anyone else in the union ever said, "Pay the great players five million a year, make the average salary one million, and the minimum a hundred thousand." They did not have to. Those present conditions grew naturally from the reforms that were introduced in 1970 and 1975.

One obvious change to this whipsaw system would have been to trade arbitration for total free agency. Miller writes that Charlie Finley proposed just that strategy to flood (so to speak) the labor market with players, thus diminishing their value. Finley was in such disapproval with the owners that he was rejected outright. Miller says that he held his breath lest someone like Walter O'Malley see that Finley was right.

The problem with total free agency for an owner like O'Malley is that some clubs, including the Dodgers, invest more than others in player development. As we have seen when looking at expansion, the attachment to players that an organization has developed itself can be quite strong. Some of the owners may have been obtuse, but it is doubtful that O'Malley was one of them. More likely, he was unwilling to spend money to develop players for other organizations.

From the Seitz decision to the present, the threat of losing games from a work stoppage has come from the owners. Even the strikes of 1981 and 1985 were triggered by the owners, as the players refused to agree to rollbacks in the gains that they had made. The union points out the obvious: that players do not receive huge pay increases at the point of a gun. Some owner or another has agreed to the worth of Player X, and the echoes through salary arbitration are simply the result of a system that the owners had accepted in contract negotiations.

When asked if he would favor total free agency, Marvin Miller tells the Finley story and slyly avoids a direct answer.[11] He points out that he never told the owners that arbitration alone would satisfy the union's objections to the players' condition. Arbitration might ease the problem of low salaries, but only free agency would meet the demands of the union that the players enjoy fundamental commercial rights in selecting their employer.

By agreeing to limit free agency to players with six years in the major leagues, the union restricted the number of players that the owners could pursue in any one year. Theoretically, their value would increase, and the players with fewer than six years' experience could enjoy a coattail effect through arbitration.

The one concession that the players have given the owners is to let eligibility for arbitration move from two years to three. The owners are free to set the salary of their youngest players subject to the new minimum of $100,000. The catch-22 continues as the owners hold the salaries of young stars far below what they would get in arbitration or on the market. The owners claim they have to hold these salaries down to recover some of the expenses that will hit when the player inherits his full rights. But the behavior also increases the militancy of the players, who chafe under this vestige of the old system, and it pressures the union to bargain for stiff hikes in the minimum salary.

Through the remainder of the Kuhn years, the owners howled at the reckless course of their business. They turned to Peter Ueberroth to save them from themselves and bring to baseball the business sense that he had displayed in running the 1984 Summer Olympics. Ueberroth solved some of their problems and significantly increased their revenues. But he will be remembered as the architect of collusion, and the owners who had appeared to be arrogant, abusive, and stubborn now followed a new strategy. And it made them appear pathetic.

The decision not to bid on free agents during the 1985–87 seasons was a stark admission by the owners of their inability to run their clubs rationally. Free market economic theory, what the owners doubtless extoll in principle, would predict that teams would bid at the margin for available players. When Tim Raines became available, Montreal would have offered perhaps a 5% salary increase. Kansas City might have proposed an 8% hike, with the Dodgers or the Yankees offering perhaps 7% more plus the commercial advantages of playing in one of those larger markets. But free agency has never worked that way.

The owners treat free agency not by the model of Adam Smith but by the example of a drunken sailor who cannot imbibe moderately once he had begun to drink. Recognizing their weakness, the owners, under the sway of Peter Ueberroth, took the pledge: no more spending on free agents.

Indeed, if the owners had risen at a meeting, sworn to leave one another's players alone, and taken an oath of *omerta* to conceal the plot, one could have a perverse kind of respect akin to the fascination we have with a good gangster movie. Instead, like a band of children caught in the act, the owners denied any wrongdoing even while their faces and hands were smeared with chocolate frosting.

The players union excoriated the owners for reneging on the 1985 Basic Agreement, a contract that expressly forbade concerted action to limit free agent opportunities. The final sentence in Article XVIII, Section H, reads, "Players shall not act in concert with other Players and Clubs shall not act in concert with other Clubs." The language had originally been included at the owners' insistence to prevent the type of tandem bargaining that Koufax and Drysdale had employed.

The union filed grievances with an arbitrator for the three seasons (1985–87) during which the owners slowed the salary spiral. Once again, the owners relied on a narrow technical defense that might have persuaded a judge, though even that is doubtful, but certainly had little chance of convincing anyone who could search for truth and justice without observing the baroque requirements of American jurisprudence.

The owners' position, which Ueberroth continues to insist is correct, is that the clubs never acted in concert. At no time did anyone suggest that all teams stop bidding for free agents. The explanation for why the clubs' behavior changed so dramatically is that Ueberroth had the clubs open their books in 1985 to expose the folly of earlier player decisions. Faced with a public display of poor judgment, teams independently decided to restrain themselves from pursuing free agents.

To fans and sportswriters, the owners' explanation was incredible. Players like Raines, Kirk Gibson, Carlton Fisk, and Jack Morris, who had records that suggested they could turn a club around, received no offers when they went on the market. Their old clubs then lowered previously offered salaries, and the free hand of the old days was restored—for the moment. Marvin Miller aptly pointed out that if players behaved in an equivalent way they would be accused of throwing games, so Miller claimed that collusion represented an even more egregious corruption than the Black Sox scandal.

The owners challenged the union to reveal "the smoking gun," and the union replied that the circumstantial evidence was sufficient and overwhelming. The arbitrators held extensive hearings and examined the evidence with great care, taking years to sort through all the allegations.

In each case, the arbitrators found for the players. Point by point, the arbitrators rejected the owners' contention that they had reached the same point independently. As arbitrator Thomas Roberts concluded, "The right of the clubs to participate in the free agency provisions of the Basic Agreement no longer remained an individual matter to be determined solely for the benefit of each club. The contemplated benefit of a common goal was substituted."[12]

The penalties for collusion offset some of the savings the owners enjoyed when they ignored the free agents. But the fines were only part of the effects of collusion with which the owners would have to live.

They had confirmed every worst suspicion of the union about the owners' trustworthiness. Every owner—from the ones who are decent and intelligent to the ones who are grasping and myopic—went along with a course of action that violated a contract that they had just signed. Their best defense was the lame explanation that Ueberroth and George Steinbrenner would offer: that lawyers were present at all meetings to make sure that nothing improper was mentioned. That may be a good technical defense in court, but it is also the best evidence that collusion was the very purpose of those owners meetings.

Recently, the facts of collusion have become clearer, and they only make the owners' position all the weaker. Peter Bavasi continues to resist the word *collusion* for the reasons Ueberroth has mentioned: the owners did not agree to a specific action in concert.[13] The former commissioner told the *Sporting News,* "I think the owners operate like sheep. Sheep go in one direction or another."[14]

That flattering portrait is one with which Bavasi agrees. He remembers that neither Ueberroth nor anyone else directly called for a strategy of not bidding on free agents. Instead, Ueberroth embarrassed the owners personally and individually about their previous spending habits. He preached the gospel of "fiscal responsibility," and collusion followed.

Bavasi says that the owners were chastened by these meetings and the fraternal humiliation that they endured. In that climate, a month went by with no bids for free agents. Waiting for someone else to break ranks, another month passed with no offers. No one ever said, "Hey, let's collude!" No one had to—sheep know what they have to do.

The result was a radical, immoral, and illegal challenge to the status quo. The owners' part was to timidly follow a commissioner who had been hired to save them from themselves. The bullies had been successfully confronted by the union, and they now were reduced to piling lie upon lie in a futile attempt to deflect the charges that their conduct was squalid.

Each of the twenty-six major league clubs now has to pay about $10 million apiece to a fund that will be divided among the players who were bypassed during the collusion years. The sum is especially burdensome to franchises like the Seattle Mariners that are struggling and hardly need the burden of paying for the practices of a previous owner.

Collusion proved to be costly to both players and owners, but as a strategy for reversing the course of salaries or blunting the power of the union, it was a failure. The next opportunity for the owners to stem the tide was the Basic Agreement of 1990. Their approach was more honest than was collusion, but the plan was poorly conceived and executed.

With barely three months left before the start of the season, the owners' Player Relations Committee (PRC) proposed a radical change in compensation. Salary arbitration would be abolished, salaries would be based on a pay-for-performance scale that would tie a player's salary to statistical criteria, salary caps would be imposed, and revenue sharing would cover all salaries, with players receiving approximately half of baseball's revenues from some but not all income sources.

Some aspects of the proposal are worthy of years of study and discussion (which is now being done); but as a bargaining position introduced weeks before pitchers and catchers reported for spring training, the offer was bizarre. Did the owners think that the union might really accept some version of that package? Was the offer an attempt to provoke a work stoppage that might rally fans to the owners' side? What did the proposals indicate about the owners' understanding of their status?

The owners' proposals were presented by Bud Selig. He has long championed the cause of clubs in small markets, explaining passionately, if not successfully, the problems that smaller franchises have in keeping up with more prosperous clubs when pursuing free agents. By running one of the leanest organizations in the game, the Brewers have been able to turn a profit.

The package that Selig offered was a desperate attempt to change the terms of the debate. It showed that at least some of the owners sincerely believed that they faced serious problems, but it also showed that the owners were still out of touch with their situation.

Selig spoke at one point about discussing the ideas for changing the Basic Agreement with Bart Giamatti, the late commissioner who had died suddenly in 1989. Giamatti had apparently encouraged Selig in a fine example of the fortress mentality at work. But the opinion that mattered was Donald Fehr's, Miller's successor as head of the players union. Despite the turmoil of the past and the need to heal the bitterness of collusion, the owners thought to talk to the union about labor relations only in the weeks before the expiration of the Basic Agreement.

The owners knew that they wanted changes in the existing relationship with the union, but they did not seem to understand that they had been replaced by the union in the role of defending the status quo. Selig was now in the position that Marvin Miller had occupied years before, trying to win major benefits through a radical overhaul of the labor relations system.

Miller's task had been daunting, but far easier than Selig's. In the 1960s, Miller could point to actual conditions that players endured and to the discrepancy between those restrictions and the prevailing American standards about fairness. Selig was forced to discuss potential problems that might occur, a theme that owners and commissioners had sounded for years in the face of greater profits than ever.

Miller had to ask a few wealthy players to stand by the many as a way to increase all their salaries. Selig had to ask phenomenally wealthy franchises like the Yankees to sacrifice tens of millions of dollars in local broadcast revenues for the benefit of teams the Yankees were trying to beat. Steinbrenner sang a few bars of "Solidarity Forever," but the dissonance was evident.

Selig's plan was doomed from the first. The union rejected it outright and countered with its own demand that arbitration rights be restored to players with two years' experience. The owners dropped their reforms like ballast on a sinking ship, but they dug in on the arbitration proposal from the union. The number of players affected by the issue was small, but the impetus that would go to either side with the appearance of a victory was as important as ever.

The owners refused to open spring training camps, damaging local economies in Florida and Arizona. The lockout received national media attention as the season openers appeared threatened. After exhausting deliberations, a compromise was reached that split the difference on the arbitration issue but also set up a panel to consider reforms for the future.

An interesting point as the owners and the union study issues of revenue sharing is whether the union is any more serious than the owners used to be when they studied reforms of the reserve clause.

In addition to the study commission, a potentially important change in labor relations occurred in the 1990 negotiations. As difficult as the bargaining was, the personal animosity that had made earlier disputes so tiresome was largely absent. The owners were represented by Charles O'Connor, who maintained a professional demeanor, as did Donald Fehr. The union chief says that the labor climate is better now but that things are still too tenuous to reach any conclusions about the future.[15]

Fehr is still unconvinced that any major league franchise faces a clear economic problem. He says that the troubles of small-market franchises that Bud Selig has brought up "are totally lacking in evidentiary support." Financial strains are thought by the union chief to be related to local conditions that are likely to be temporary.

The obstacles to a radical change in the Basic Agreement are clear when Fehr is asked about the union's willingness to consider total free agency as a substitute for arbitration. Fehr says he is willing to consider the possibility of phasing in such a change, but it would have to be preceded by an elimination of the amateur draft. In effect, the union would want to extend free agency to the amateur ranks. The end of the draft would be difficult for the small-market teams to accept because the draft was introduced to limit the ability of the Dodgers and the Yankees to capture a preponderance of young talent.

The lockout ended with calls for a new era in labor relations, specifically a partnership between players and owners. The partnership is a complete fiction if the union does not share with the owners the authority to make revenue decisions. Expansion, broadcasting contracts, and other matters now completely in the owners' control would have to be shared. The prospect is another test for the owners' ability to adjust to the new realities of their business. Based on past performance, the partnership is a long way off.

NOTES

1. Buzzie Bavasi, *Off the Record* (Chicago: Contemporary Books, 1987), p. 103.
2. Ibid, p. 104.
3. Don Drysdale, with Bob Verdi, *Once a Bum, Always a Dodger: My Life in Baseball from Brooklyn to Los Angeles* (New York: St. Martin's Press, 1990), p. 132.
4. Ibid, p. 131.
5. Kuhn, *Hardball*, p. 77.
6. *Sporting News*, July 21, 1991, p. 10.
7. Lee MacPhail, *My Nine Innings: An Autobiography of Fifty Years in Baseball* (Westport, Conn.: Meckler Books, 1989), p. 101.

THE DIAMOND REVOLUTION

8. Kenneth Jennings, *Balls and Strikes: The Money Game in Professional Baseball* (New York: Praeger, 1990), p. 26.
9. Kuhn, *Hardball*, p. 141.
10. MacPhail, *My Nine Innings*, pp. 101–2.
11. Miller interview.
12. In the Matter of the Arbitration Between Major League Baseball Players Association and the Twenty-Six Major League Baseball Clubs, the Matters Put at Issue By Grievance No. 86-2., Sept. 21, 1987.
13. Bavasi interview.
14. *Sporting News,* July 29, 1991, p. 10.
15. Fehr interview.

9

Leading
the Revolution

The first phase of a revolution is the fun part. Youthful enthusiasm dumps tea in Boston Harbor or dances atop the
Berlin Wall before pulverizing it into souvenirs of the cold
war at ten dollars a chunk. The more difficult phase of a
radical transition is establishing the new regime. False starts,
cries of betrayal, predictions of doom, and endless disputes
about minor items characterize the creation of the new order.

The next era for baseball will likely take one of two distinct
paths. In the optimistic scenario, the popularity of the game
continues to expand. More and more people are captivated by
the charms of the game. Attendance rises, television viewing
increases, licensed products become even more fashionable,
and more youngsters play the game. The revenue flow continues to increase, sustaining even higher salaries that draw
even more athletes to choose baseball as their career.

With diligence and imagination, the technological and cultural bridges to an international game are constructed. Baseball rivals soccer as an international sport with greater
popularity than ever in America. Teams retain a national character, but players are free to sign with the club that makes the
best offer regardless of country. The financial base of this
international game is almost impossible to comprehend, and

THE DIAMOND REVOLUTION

the prosperity of the business reaches a spectacular level. Or perhaps not.

The alternate course is that the revenue stream contracts. The next television package is lower than the current one. Families spend their entertainment money elsewhere. Ticket prices are beyond the reach of the average fan, so attendance drops while clubs try to sustain the same income from a smaller pool.

Perhaps hockey will solve its marketing problems and become the new fashion in sport. Baseball caps and shirts continue to sell, but one sees more logos of the Rangers than the Mets, the Kings more than the Dodgers. The NBA and the NFL continue to fight hard for the money in licensed products, and baseball is unable to squeeze any advantage over the other major sports.

Like a real estate bubble that bursts, a few owners decide to get out, but they have trouble finding buyers. The offers that are made are for tens of millions less than what the current owner had paid. Operating losses climb even after the front office has started to run like a serious business rather than as a hobby. Attempts to control the drain of player salaries trigger more strikes and lockouts that drive the fans even further from the game.

The international game never develops. Like soccer in the United States, pockets of enthusiasm remain isolated. The development of baseball falls back in Europe, and the quality of play in Asia and Latin America never approaches major league caliber.

A key factor in determining the course of baseball's future will be leadership, and that is a very problematic matter. The essence of the diamond revolution has been to turn a feudal industry into a modern market, and that transition means that crucial decisions are no longer determined solely by the preferences of the owners. Some of the new owners may have baronial pretensions, but their former peasants are now prosperous and free. Choices today are made by voluntary agreements between players and owners after deliberations that sometimes have been bitter.

A market system is especially interesting when applied to baseball. The market, like a democracy, will deliver what its participants demand, and what we demand reflects our understanding of our self-interest. In Adam Smith's famous construction, the sum of individual calculations of self-interest operate as an "invisible hand" to guide society to the best outcome for the entire community.

Certainly within the community of baseball, the rhetorical support for market theory is enthusiastic. From Donald Fehr to Fay Vincent, the market is extolled as the best mechanism for making economic choices. Players salaries, expansion fees, broadcast rights, and other payments arc justified as the product of decisions that have been reached freely by the most interested parties. This faith in the market is ardent, but closer examination shows important discrepancies between the reality of the baseball business and the theory of the market.

To begin with, the assumption that the pursuit of self-interest yields the best outcome for the group begs the questions Who is the self in baseball, and what is its interest? On the face of it, baseball has no coherent self, for in its commercial dimension there is neither a consensus among its several participants nor a definitive authority to force a single interest on fractious parties.

Bowie Kuhn displayed a common confusion about the cohesion within baseball in his treatment of the Curt Flood case. Kuhn described the district court's ruling with the words, "On August 12, Judge Cooper ruled in favor of *baseball* [emphasis added]."[1] Kuhn's book uses that expression at a number of points. But if Bowie Kuhn was baseball, what was Curt Flood? Kuhn, and every other commissioner, is hired by the major league owners ostensibly to promote the best interests of the game, but the limitations in realizing that goal are inescapable. The Flood case demonstrated that within the community of baseball there has always been a fundamental division over the interests of the business in terms of labor relations.

Kuhn could effectively represent the owners' position, and he no doubt was sincere in so doing. What he could not do was speak on behalf of "baseball." If that claim had been valid, he would not have been in court in the first place. The judge did not rule in favor of baseball; he ruled in favor of one of the powerful factions within the game. That the other powerful faction, the union, ultimately won free agency shows how hollow "baseball's" judicial victory was.

Since baseball, per se, does not have a discernible self-interest, what kind of cohesion exists within the groups of players and owners?

As we have seen, the union has displayed remarkable solidarity. Superstars who make millions of dollars per year have sacrificed for those making the minimum salary. Players at the end of their career have stood with rookies. Unlike Peter Ueberroth's characterization of the owners, the players have not been sheep. They have listened carefully to what Marvin Miller and Donald Fehr have told them. They have trusted these men, and they have settled internal differences within the union.

The owners, on the other hand, seem to split at times into twenty-six separate groups. Large market–small market tensions receive a great deal of attention, but that may not be the critical division because the Yankees and the Brewers can eventually figure out how to split gate and media revenues as needed. More intractable is the difference in the ways that clubs use their money, the ways that they perceive their interests given the circumstances of their own market.

None of the owners openly avows a policy of trying to buy a championship, but clearly that has been tried in some cases. The money that some teams have given free agents has exasperated the more frugal clubs. The Yankees' recent signing of

Leading the Revolution

Brien Taylor, a high school player, sent several owners into orbit. But the Yankees are not necessarily a franchise that will simply throw money at championships. Strong evidence suggests that the money that George Steinbrenner spent on free agents was an eminently prudent investment.

The world championships that the Yankees won in 1977 and 1978 revived the most famous franchise in baseball. For a decade, the club had been as bad as any in baseball, while the Mets became the darlings of New York. By opening his checkbook in the early years of free agency, Steinbrenner bypassed the slow and uncertain path of developing young prospects. Was the free spending financially imprudent?

If the Yankees' cable deal is considered as a return on the free agent investments, the team's spending has been returned many times over. What may have been a personal indulgence for Steinbrenner may also have been an extremely wise investment. For a few million dollars in salaries over a five-year stretch, the Yankees were able to secure half a billion dollars in revenue for twelve seasons.

Steinbrenner's relationship with Billy Martin could be a case study in an abnormal psych textbook. His bullying of clerical staff was inexcusable. His dealings with Howard Spira were reprehensible. But the money that he spent, he got back—many times over.

The point is not that the Steinbrenner model of ownership is the one that all clubs should follow. Rather, a successful financial operation in New York may require different decisions than those that would be made in Cincinnati or Pittsburgh, and that is precisely the owners' problem. Even the Autry family now forswears running the team as a hobby. Every owner, without sliding back into collusion, could independently decide to be fiscally prudent; it would not matter. Fiscal prudence simply means different things in different markets:

- How many games will be televised?
- Over-the-air or cable?

- Will beer be shut off after the sixth inning or the eighth?
- Will you pay a million dollars for a high school kid?
- Will a Mariners move to St. Petersburg be allowed?
- How elaborate should your scouting department be?
- Should the leagues expand again?
- What about interleague play?
- Realignment?
- Wild-card playoffs?

The owners will have to decide each of these questions, and many similar ones besides. And they will have the Devil's own time reaching decisions because they lack the kind of common perspective that the players share.

The owners' problem is not so much that some of them want to win and hang the expense while others insist that a budget be respected even if it costs a pennant. All of the owners want to win and also make money. But the avenues to pennants and prosperity are different for each franchise. In other words, for purposes of market transactions, the owners lack a coherent self.

The players by comparison have relatively simple questions to answer. Marvin Miller assured the high-salaried players that they would make several times more money if they allied with their less wealthy teammates. He was proven correct, and ever since it has been relatively easy to keep the players together. They have found that acting in concert pays great returns for each and every one of them.

With respect to the interests of these two factions, these economic selves, the players again have all the best of it. Their interest is to secure as much money as they possibly can right now. Marvin Miller has been criticized by commissioners and owners for lacking an appreciation for the greater interests of baseball, for its long-term future. But Miller can reply that as the market theory predicts, the future will take care of itself if the proper decisions are made today. For the interests that he represented, Miller held up his end of the business.

Leading the Revolution

The union, in fact, can operate from a longer perspective than individual players might have. Since the players have a paramount interest in making as much money as they can during their brief careers, they may be disposed to economic decisions that create long-range problems. As an institution, the union must consider its future that will extend beyond the careers of the current players, so, to a degree at least, the more extreme impulses of the players might be modified by their union.

The owners have more complicated choices to make than the players. Almost any athlete will try to stay in the game as long as possible. But an owner might be in and out of baseball in less time than a journeyman shortstop's career. A single championship, frustration with his colleagues, or financial reversals in his other businesses might drive an owner from the game in just a few years. Depending on how long the owner plans to stay, decisions about revenues will be perceived differently.

Owners can make their money through both annual operating profits and equity when they sell the club. Some will decide to forgo money this season to build the value of the franchise over the long haul. The distinction between immediate revenues and long-term value will affect decisions about stadiums, relocation, and expansion. Again, the players face no such complications.

The advantages in cohesion and clarity that the union has over the owners do not preclude potential pitfalls for the players. Irving Kristol's point about the Horatio Alger myths is pertinent here. As beneficiaries of baseball's popularity, the players have an interest in seeing that the game remains appreciated by the public, but that may not happen if grasping materialism is the only evident value.

The players and the owners demonstrate two potential problems with the market. The owners have been too fractured to play the economic game successfully, and the players may be getting what they want but not necessarily what they need—hence the critical role of leadership.

213

THE DIAMOND REVOLUTION

*   *   *

Commissioner Fay Vincent has spent much of his professional life in the entertainment business, both with baseball and with Columbia Pictures. When asked if the American economy puts too much of its resources into entertainment at the expense of more essential pursuits, Vincent rejects the suggestion.[2] Not surprisingly, he professes that the market sorts those choices out better than any other method. But the commissioner does see potential damage that can arise through the market when he discusses players' salaries.

Vincent draws a parallel with the American steel industry, which he thinks is suffering because of excessive compensation to its workers. The Steelworkers Union secured those salaries through a collective bargaining process, but, as Vincent sees it, the industry has struggled to remain competitive in a global economy because of those agreements.

Somewhat resignedly, the commissioner allows that something like that could occur in baseball. An economic contraction that would pummel weaker franchises is a possibility. But concluding that financial distress is the result of a union's success misses a larger point.

For most of the history of both the steel industry and baseball, the owners lived like royalty at the expense of the workers. When workers found that they could improve their lot by organizing and bargaining collectively, they pressed the same cultural values that their employers had revered: immediate returns and consumption. By contrast, the Japanese have sacrificed some of their standard of living in order to build the savings to drive their economy.

The threat to baseball's prosperity is less who wins the battles between players and owners and more that the nature of the battles themselves becomes too tedious and sterile for the fans to tolerate. Don Fehr emphatically rejects the argument that the public is weary of the financial wrangling.[3] He notes that the game has never been more popular than during these years of economic strife.

Leading the Revolution

Whether the popularity has grown because of or in spite of the front office wars is a critical question. Attempts to organize fan boycotts after strikes and lockouts have been complete busts, but it is hard to see what the public could possibly find interesting about the recent tilts between players and owners.

When the issues turned on the reserve clause and players' rights to work where they choose, most fans could appreciate the union's point because that right is fundamental in this country. With free agency secured and the issues refined to a fine-tuning of arbitration eligibility and the owners' pipe dreams of a different system, it is harder for most of us to appreciate why we are deprived of the games by a lockout or a strike.

Leadership will be essential in determining whether baseball's newly emerging market advances a rational and enlightened self-interest or becomes a babble of atomistic indulgence. To promote the more sensible course, reforms in the leadership of baseball are needed.

The problem as things stand is that baseball has two chief executives, the commissioner and the union chief. The commissioner enjoys certain superficial symbols that suggest that he is the head of major league baseball. In fact, much of his actual power has been lost in independent arbitration, and his persuasive ability is limited by the knowledge that the commissioner's most immediate constituency is the owners.

Most commissioners from the time of Judge Landis have battled club owners and secured the authority of the office over the franchises to determine the best interests of baseball. The personal integrity of the commissioners has not been an issue, but the flawed structure of the office and the rise of importance in the Players Association have rendered the commissionership too weak to lead the revolution.

The din of two strong voices has complicated critical issues such as labor relations, disciplinary matters, and expansion.

215

Not only does the public become confused, but, more important, the development of sound policies in those areas is seriously compromised.

The problems of a plural executive were a subject of Federalist Paper No. 70, and Alexander Hamilton could have been writing as aptly about the commissionership of a game that was then in its embryonic form.

> Whenever two or more persons are engaged in any common enterprise or pursuit, there is always danger of difference of opinion. If it be a public trust or office in which they are clothed with equal dignity and authority, there is peculiar danger of personal emulation and even animosity. From either, and especially from all these causes, the most bitter dissensions are apt to spring. Whenever these happen, they lessen the respectability, weaken the authority, and distract the plans and operations of those whom they divide. . . . And what is still worse, they might split the community into the most violent and irreconcilable factions, adhering differently to the different individuals who composed the magistracy.[4]

The "bitter dissensions" that Hamilton mentions are a fitting description of the relationship between Marvin Miller and Bowie Kuhn. Their differences became personal and continued even to the memoirs that each wrote when they retired from their responsibilities. The head of the union and the commissioner become focal points around whom the contending factions can organize.

In the politics of baseball, the union has become as important and powerful as the owners, and the commissioner's office needs to reflect this change. The most obvious adjustment that must be made is to have the commissioner represent both parties. In their own minds at least, the individuals who have held the office have tried to do just that, but the structure of the job frustrates those efforts.

The present arrangement makes no more sense than limiting voting to Republicans and being satisfied that their choice will be equally concerned about the interests of Democrats. Even if such is the case, the appearance alone is too troubling to let stand.

One possible mechanism for the selection of future commissioners is to establish a committee of two owners and two union officials that would review prospective candidates and nominate one unanimously. The nominee would have to win the approval of one-half plus one of the club owners of each league and the same majority from the players, voting by team.

Recognizing that this selection affects other parties, such as umpires and the minor leagues, those groups should have an opportunity to testify before the nominating committee about potential candidates. The reality is that neither the minor leagues nor the umpires is of comparable power to the players and the owners, so their role in the selection process is correspondingly diminished.

The obvious danger with this proposal is that choosing a commissioner would become another battleground between players and owners. So it might be, but facts militate against that. The simple act of adopting such a system would signify some progress in the owners' acceptance of parity with the players. Why agree to the change if you intend to be uncooperative?

Another consideration is that equal voting power effectively gives each faction a veto over the other. The insistence that a biased candidate be selected would be futile, so the parties would have an institutional incentive to select an individual who is at least acceptable to both sides.

The policies that must be made to respond to the challenges of the future could follow a similar procedure as the selection process. The commissioner, in consultation with the experts in his office, could recommend actions on media contracts, expansion, franchise moves, and other matters, with the recommendations subject to ratification by the owners and the players.

This reform would strengthen the central authority of the commissioner's office over the individual clubs, and that might cause some alarm among the more powerful owners. But they can consider that their prosperity depends on the stability of the weaker franchises, and the future of baseball depends on its advance as a coherent community.

Before suggesting specific policies for baseball to follow in the future, this refashioned commissioner's office should clarify the values that will guide its deliberations. Fundamentally, baseball should decide to grow slowly and patiently, rejecting the impulse to grab the quick buck.

To that end, decisions should be biased in favor of tradition over innovation, because the heritage of the game is a great resource but one that could be squandered by fashion. Leadership should be exercised through example so that tinny calls for sacrifice do not follow an orgy of self-indulgence. Finally, the new leadership must continually invest in the game's base of support: Family entertainment should take precedence over corporate perks; playgrounds for kids should come before new stadiums; and minor leagues and high school and college ball should be supported as needed.

From the perspective of those values, specific measures can be proposed for some of the topics considered in this book.

- *Race*—Without imposing numerical targets that must be met, the commissioner should stress to the clubs that they can safely assume on the basis of history that minority and female talent is being wasted. Until better results are achieved with hiring for the front office, no club should make the argument that it is doing all it can but still losing money.
- *Franchise Moves*—No. If an owner wants to relocate to another community, he or she should sell the club and buy a new one. The record is clear that there have been bad owners but not bad baseball towns.
- *Stadiums*—Teams should play in baseball-only, grass, open-air facilities that have been financed predominantly by

the ball clubs. For the sake of tradition, Fenway Park and Wrigley Field must be retained even if the Red Sox and the Cubs need to receive a subsidy to compensate for whatever financial sacrifice that might impose.

• *Expansion*—Expansion to thirty-two teams should proceed at once, and future expansion should seriously consider the upgrading of minor leagues rather than the addition of new teams. The season should be returned to 154 games, with no wild-card teams in the playoffs.

• *The Small-Market Problem*—Before any money is transferred to struggling franchises, the commissioner's office should send management assistants to make sure that the franchise is being operated as efficiently as possible.

• *Television and Radio*—New technology should be facilitated. Revenues should be secured primarily through the development of attractive viewing and listening packages with a limited complementary role for punitive fines for unauthorized reception. International markets should be promoted.

• *Labor Relations*—Drop salary arbitration in favor of extended free agency. If the union can participate sufficiently in management responsibilities to have a fair influence, then sharing profits and losses could supplement salaries that could be structured or capped by mutual agreement.

These measures might very well cost baseball some money in the short run. Clubs that operate on the margin and players near the end of their career would have special sacrifices to make. But their financial losses would be directed to the greater prosperity of the entire business. The zero-sum game between players and owners would be replaced by a cooperative venture that appreciates the potential for the equity of the ball club and even higher pensions if the future growth of the business is secured.

Making the commissioner a more representative figure and providing him staff support to keep abreast of this complex business is no panacea. Even placing a talented and energetic person in the job to persuade the various interests in the game to keep larger purposes in mind will not be sufficient to secure a prosperous future for baseball.

Responsible behavior cannot be deposited in one office and ignored elsewhere. All the parties in baseball must cooperate to promote some fundamental values. The recent history of baseball is dominated by expedient and cynical behavior that virtually precludes trust and cooperation. The major league owners are primarily responsible for that condition because of their inexcusable collusion on free agents. But the union must be careful that it does not emulate the thing it abhors.

Even though the owners raised narrow material gain to an overriding interest, the union must resist any impulse to follow suit. That may not be easy because the Players Association seems able to clobber the owners at will. But the bridge to a prosperous future as an international game is a high road that has no place for the squabbles of the past.

We fans will also need to be more responsible in making sure that we keep this wonderful game in proper perspective. Not even a seventh game of the World Series is as important as playing catch with our children. Not even the most magnificent ball park should be a source of community pride if suffering people have been neglected to pay for it. Not even extra innings on a hot summer day justifies letting fans become dangerous drunks.

The turmoil in the business of baseball has included a greater awareness of the abuses in the game that were long ignored. Free agency, alcohol treatment, community relations, expansion, more stable franchises, and revived minor leagues are some of the impressive steps that baseball has taken to keep apace of its times.

The next generation of baseball will see its share of commercial and legal battles, but solid evidence should encourage us that the game is in good shape. With sound leadership and an appreciation for the enduring values of the game, our grandchildren will look back at this turbulent time as the emergence of the international pastime.

NOTES

1. Kuhn, *Hardball*, p. 87.
2. Fay Vincent, interview, Vincent's office, July 17, 1991.
3. Donald Fehr, interview, Fehr's office, June 24, 1991.
4. *The Federalist Papers*, edited by Clinton Rossiter (New York: New American Library, 1961), pp. 425–26.

Bibliography

I—BOOKS

Aaron, Henry, with Lonnie Wheeler. *I Had A Hammer: The Hank Aaron Story.* New York: HarperCollins, 1991.

Alexander, Charles. *Our Game: An American Baseball History.* New York: Holt, 1991.

Baseball America. *The Baseball Draft: The First 25 Years.* Durham, N.C.: American Sports, 1990.

Bavasi, Buzzie, with John Strege. *Off the Record.* Chicago: Contemporary Books, 1987.

Baylor, Don with Claire Smith. *Don Baylor: Nothing But the Truth—Baseball Life.* New York: St. Martin's Press, 1989.

Berry, Robert C., William G. Gould IV, and Paul D. Staudohar. *Labor Relations in Professional Sports.* Dover, Mass.: Auburn House, 1986.

Berry, Robert C., and Glenn M. Wong. *Law and Business of the Sports Industries.* vols. I and II. Dover, Mass.: Auburn House, 1986.

Bouton, Jim. *Ball Four: My Life and Hard Times Throwing the Knuckleball in the Big Leagues.* New York: World, 1970.

Chandler, Happy, with Vance Trimble. *Heroes, Plain Folks and Skunks: The Life and Times of Happy Chandler.* Chicago: Bonus Books, 1989.

Drysdale, Don, with Bob Verdi. *Once a Bum, Always a Dodger: My Life in Baseball from Brooklyn to Los Angeles.* New York: St. Martin's Press, 1990.

Dworkin, James B. *Owners Versus Players: Baseball and Collective Bargaining.* Dover, Mass.: Auburn House, 1981.

Falkner, David. *The Nine Sides of the Diamond: Baseball's Great Glove Men on the Fine Art of Defense.* New York: Random House, 1990.

Gammons, Peter. *Beyond the Sixth Game.* Boston: Houghton Mifflin, 1985.

Halberstam, David. *Summer of '49.* New York: Morrow, 1989.

Bibliography

Hall, Donald, with Dock Ellis. *Dock Ellis: In the Country of Baseball*. New York: Fireside, 1989.

Honig, Donald. *Baseball America: The Heroes of the Game and the Times of Their Glory*. New York: Macmillan, 1985.

Howe, Steve, with Jim Greenfield. *Between the Lines: One Athlete's Struggle to Escape the Nightmare of Addiction*. Grand Rapids, Mich.: Masters Press, 1989.

Klatell, David A., and Norman Marcus. *Sports for Sale: Television, Money and the Fans*. New York: Oxford University Press, 1988.

Kubek, Tony, and Terry Pluto. *Sixty-One: The Team, the Record, the Men*. New York: Fireside, 1987.

James, Bill. *The Bill James Historical Baseball Abstract*. New York: Villard, 1986.

Jennings, Kenneth M. *Balls and Strikes: The Money Game in Professional Baseball*. New York: Praeger, 1990.

Lowenfish, Lee. *The Imperfect Diamond*, rev. ed. New York: Da Capo Press, 1991.

Macmillan. *The Baseball Encyclopedia: The Complete and Official Record of Major League Baseball*, 3rd ed. New York: Macmillan, 1976.

MacPhail, Lee. *My Nine Innings: An Autobiography of Fifty Years in Baseball*. Westport, Conn.: Meckler Books, 1989.

Mantle, Mickey, with Herb Gluck. *The Mick: An American Hero: The Legend and the Glory*. New York: Doubleday, 1985.

Markham, Jesse W., and Paul V. Teplitz. *Baseball Economics and Public Policy*. Lexington, Mass.: Lexington Books, 1981.

Mays, Willie, with Lou Sahadi. *Say Hey: The Autobiography of Willie Mays*. New York: Simon & Schuster, 1988.

Miller, James Edward. *The Baseball Business: Pursuing Pennants and Profits in Baltimore*. Chapel Hill: University of North Carolina Press, 1990.

Miller, Marvin. *A Whole Different Ball Game: The Sport and Business of Baseball*. New York: Birch Lane Press, 1991.

Okrent, Daniel. *Nine Innings*. New York: Ticknor & Fields, 1985.

O'Neil, Terry. *The Game Behind the Game: High Stakes, High Pressure in Television Sports*. New York: HarperCollins, 1989.

Peterson, Robert. *Only the Ball Was White*. New York: McGraw-Hill, 1984.

Polner, Murray. *Branch Rickey*. New York: Signet, 1982.

Robinson, Frank, and Barry Stainback. *Extra Innings*. New York: McGraw-Hill, 1988.

Rogosin, Donn. *Invisible Men: Life in Baseball's Negro Leagues*. New York: Atheneum, 1987.

Rose, Pete, and Roger Kahn. *Pete Rose: My Story*. New York: Macmillan, 1989.

Bibliography

Scully, Gerald W. *The Business of Major League Baseball*. Chicago: University of Chicago Press, 1989.

Smith, Curt. *Voices of the Game: The First Full-Scale Overview of Baseball Broadcasting, 1921 to the Present*. South Bend, Ind.: Diamond Communications, 1987.

Sullivan, Neil J. *The Dodgers Move West*. New York: Oxford University Press, 1987.

———. *The Minors: The Struggles and the Triumph of Baseball's Poor Relation from 1876 to the Present*. New York: St. Martin's Press, 1990.

Thorn, John, and John Holway. *The Pitcher*. New York: Prentice-Hall, 1987.

———. *Total Baseball*, 2d ed. New York: Warner Books, 1991.

Thrift, Syd, and Barry Shapiro. *The Game According to Syd*. New York: Simon & Schuster, 1990.

U.S. Congress. Senate. "Professional Sports Antitrust Immunity." Hearings Before the Committee on the Judiciary, 97th Cong., 2d sess., 1982.

———. House. "Professional Sports." Hearings Before the Subcommittee on Commerce, Transportation and Tourism of the Committee on Energy and Commerce, 99th Cong., 1st sess., 1985.

———. Senate. "Professional Sports Antitrust Immunity." Hearings Before the Committee on the Judiciary, 99th Cong., 1st sess., 1985.

Veeck, Bill, with Ed Linn. *The Hustler's Handbook*. New York: Fireside, 1989.

———. *Veeck as in Wreck*. New York: Fireside, 1989.

Voigt, David Q. *American Baseball: From Postwar Expansion to the Electronic Age*, vol. III. University Park: Pennsylvania State University Press, 1983.

Welch, Bob, and George Vecsey. *Five O'Clock Comes Early: A Young Man's Battle with Alcoholism*. New York: Quill, 1986.

Will, George F. *Men At Work: The Craft of Baseball*. New York: Macmillan, 1990.

Williams, Ted, with John Underwood. *My Turn at Bat: The Story of My Life*. New York: Fireside, 1988.

Wills, Maury, and Mike Celizic. *On the Run: The Never Dull and Often Shocking Life of Maury Wills*. New York: Carroll and Graf, 1991.

Wright, Craig R., and Tom House. *The Diamond Appraised*. New York: Fireside, 1989.

Zimmerman, Dennis. *The Private Use of Tax-Exempt Bonds: Controlling Public Subsidy of Private Activity*. Washington, D.C.: Urban Institute Press, 1991.

Zoss, Joel, and John Bowman. *Diamonds in the Rough: The Untold Story of Baseball*. New York: Macmillan, 1989.

Bibliography

II—JOURNALS

Baseball America
Baseball Research Journal
Sports Illustrated
Sporting News
USA Today Baseball Weekly

III—INTERVIEWS

Mark Abel, his office, September 13, 1990.
Robert Aylward, his office, August 2, 1990.
Robert Baade, his office, September 12, 1990.
Peter Bavasi, his office, June 26, 1991.
Jeff Becker, his office, August 3, 1990.
Phil Best, by telephone, September 22, 1990.
Steve Burroughs, his office, September 13, 1990.
Corey Busch, his office, August 23, 1990.
Seth Davidson, his office, August 3, 1990.
Andy Dolich, by telephone, August 23, 1990.
Donald Fehr, his office, June 24, 1991.
Fernando Ferrer, his office, September 6, 1990.
Wally Haas, his office, August 23, 1990.
Roland Hemond, his office, August 2, 1990.
Bill Johnson, by telephone, June 10, 1991.
Jaime Jarrin, Dodger Stadium, August 21, 1990.
Fred Kuhlman, his office, September 13, 1990.
Sam Katz, his office, October 1, 1990.
Mal Klein, by telephone, June 14, 1991.
Andy MacPhail, his office, June 29, 1990.
Lee MacPhail, his home, July 31, 1990.
Marvin Miller, his home, March 21, 1991.
Gene McHale, his home, September 28, 1990.
Don Newcombe, Dodger Stadium, August 21, 1990.
Debbie Neugester, her office, October 1, 1990.
David Nicoll, his office, August 3, 1990.
Peter O'Malley, his office, August 19, 1990 and August 20, 1991.
John Paley, his office, August 21, 1990.
Gabe Paul, Jr., his office, September 14, 1990.
Norman Redlech, his office, March 12, 1991.
Al Rosen, his office, August 23, 1990.

225

Bibliography

Bud Selig, his office, September 14, 1990.
Jim Sanders, his office, August 3, 1990.
Brent Schuyer, his office, August 21, 1990.
Janet Marie Smith, her office, August 2, 1990.
Chip Toma, by telephone, August 29, 1991.
Fay Vincent, his office, July 17, 1991 and July 19, 1991.
John Young, by telephone, July 3, 1991.
Dennis Zimmerman, by telephone, May 2, 1991.

Index

227

Index

Index

229

Index

Index

231

Index